NUSSBAUM, FELICITY

THE BRINK OF ALL
WE HATE

OCT 23 1987
DEC 15 1987
NOV 25 1988
DEC 09 1988
JUN 8 1998

The Brink of All We Hate

The Brink of All We Hate

English Satires on Women
1660-1750

Felicity A. Nussbaum

THE UNIVERSITY PRESS OF KENTUCKY

For RENE, MARC, and NICOLE

Scholarly publisher for the Commonwealth,
serving Bellarmine College, Berea College, Centre
College of Kentucky, Eastern Kentucky University,
The Filson Club, Georgetown College, Kentucky
Historical Society, Kentucky State University,
Morehead State University, Murray State University,
Northern Kentucky University, Transylvania University,
University of Kentucky, University of Louisville,
and Western Kentucky University.

Editorial and Sales Offices: Lexington, Kentucky 40506-0024

Library of Congress Cataloging in Publication Data

Nussbaum, Felicity. 1944–
    The brink of all we hate.

    Includes bibliographical references.
    1. Women in literature. 2. English literature—18th
century—History and criticism. 3. English literature—
Early modern, 1500-1700—History and criticism.
4. Satire, English—History and criticism. I. Title.
PR449.W65N87 1983   827'.4'09352042   83-10181
ISBN 0-8131-1498-5

Contents

Ladies, like variegated Tulips, show;
'Tis to their Changes that their charms they owe;
Their happy Spots the nice admirer take,
Fine by defect, and delicately weak.
'Twas thus Calypso once each heart alarm'd,
Aw'd without Virtue, without Beauty charm'd;
Her Tongue bewitch'd as odly as her Eyes,
Less Wit than Mimic, more a Wit than wise:
Strange graces still, and stranger flights she had,
Was just not ugly, and was just not mad;
Yet ne'er so sure our passion to create,
As when she touch'd the brink of all we hate.

—Pope, "Epistle to a Lady"

Acknowledgments

As a Summer Fellow at the William Andrews Clark Memorial Library in 1974 I first began to delve into the feminist controversy of the late seventeenth century, and I am grateful to Maximillian Novak for his help, as well as to the other Clark Fellows, especially Paula Backscheider and David Tarbet. This book owes its inception to discussions with my former colleague Gloria Kaufman many years ago, and I am much indebted to her for her early encouragement. Other colleagues and friends have read portions of the manuscript and offered constructive criticism and sage counsel, including Max Byrd, Steven Cohan, Jean Howard, Arthur Hoffman, Robert Hume, William Kupersmith, Roy Schreiber, Howard Weinbrot, and Mas'ud Zavarzadeh. I owe a particular debt, both intellectual and personal, to Philip B. Daghlian, who has remained a steady source of wit and inspiration. Jean Rice provided meticulous typing.

The American Council of Learned Societies supported my early research in England. I have been extremely fortunate in the generous help I have received throughout the progress of the book from the staffs of the following libraries: the Bodleian Library, Oxford; the British Library; the William Andrews Clark Memorial Library; the Cornell University libraries; the Henry E. Huntington Library; the University of Rochester Library; the Bird Library at Syracuse University; and the Yale University libraries. In the course of seeking the texts discussed in this book, I have met with unqualified courtesy. Syracuse University has provided summer research fellowships and support for preparation of this manuscript, for which I am grateful.

An earlier version of chapter 2 appeared in the publications of the Augustan Reprint Society, No. 180 (1976), William Andrews Clark Memorial Library, University of California at Los Angeles. Parts of chapter 6 appeared in "Juvenal, Swift, and *The Folly of Love*," *Eighteenth-Century Studies* 9 (1976): 540-52. And portions of chapter 8 appeared as "Pope's 'To a Lady' and the Ideal Eighteenth-Century Woman," in *Philological Quarterly* 54 (1975): 444-56. I thank the editors and publishers for permission to reprint them here.

I

Introduction

Satirists have always waged verbal warfare against the failings of mankind. They urge human nature toward reformation or simply hold the mirror up to nature to allow us to study our faults. Dryden, Rochester, Swift, and Pope, among the satirists of the Restoration and eighteenth century in England, ridicule the whole of the human race for their personal, social, moral, and political offenses. The sex of humanity is generally unspecified in satires such as Lord Rochester's "A Satyr Against Reason and Mankind" or Samuel Johnson's "The Vanity of Human Wishes," and the satirist's rhetoric mocks characteristics of humanity's precarious position between angel and beast. On the other hand, the references are specifically male when, for example, Rochester attacks Charles II's promiscuity because it causes him to neglect his duties as king. Rochester satirically compares the length of Charles's scepter and that of his sexual organ: "Poor prince! thy prick, like thy buffoons at Court / Will govern thee because it makes thee sport."[1] But the satire strikes at the peculiar aberrations of Charles II and his court wits, not at men as a sex because of their inherent lust and inconstancy. At the same time, however, most major satirists of the period address specific poems to women as a sex. According to the tradition, women deserve to be rebuked for those characteristics of their sex that make them inferior to men and make them more similar to each other than to the rest of humanity. "The Soules of women are so small / That some believe th'have none at all," Samuel Butler charges; and

Pope writes, "most Women have no Characters at all." While the number of satires against women in relation to the satirists' other works is not high (except perhaps for Rochester or Swift), what is remarkable is the persistence of the themes and the repetitiveness of the conventions. The texts selected here, though not exhaustive in scope, represent a thorough sampling of characteristic satiric *topoi* and provide a clear line of continuous antifeminist poetic portrayal throughout the Restoration and the eighteenth century.

Among the women who protest the antifeminist satiric myth in satires of the period is Laetitia Pilkington. The woman Swift calls "a d—ned, insolent, proud, unmannerly slut" contends in her *Memoirs* (1748) that women are quick to forgive men for their faults. Why, she laments, are men less willing to pardon women's flaws? "Of all things in nature, I most wonder why men should be severe in their censures on our sex, for a failure in point of chastity. Is it not monstrous that our seducers should be our accusers? Will they not employ fraud, nay, often force, to gain us? What various arts, what stratagems, what wiles will they use for our destruction?—but that once accomplished, every opprobrious term with which our language so plentifully abounds shall be bestowed on us, even by the very villains who have wronged us."[2]

This book documents and categorizes satires against women in order to isolate the conventions, to establish the ways those conventions create a recognizable satiric myth, to provide critical readings of selected poetic texts in the antifeminist tradition, and to make some generalizations about the nature of satire. In making antifeminism the center of an entire book on neoclassical satire, I am exploring the extent to which the various poets simply reiterate familiar phrases in a tradition, or, more artfully, add nuance to convey the ambivalence inherent in the female sex. The poems taken in context may then allow us to read individual poems by such satirists as Rochester, Swift, and Pope in a more informed way. Again and again modern literary critics point to aspects of this myth without penetrating the context—identifying scatological references to a woman's boudoir without noting the antecedents, or mistakenly taking conventional meta-phorical associations as evidence of an individual poet's pathology (womb/tomb, for example). The poet may be perverse or mad, but if he is, he is part of a long tradition of perversity and insanity, and the poems are more accurately read in that context.

When we determine resemblances among antifeminist satires, we can elucidate the conventions and myths which allowed satirists to catch hold of deeply disturbing elements and create a poetic fiction of power and authority. Perpetu-ating a myth which manipulates expectations between the sexes, the antifeminist satiric tradition includes not only the late seventeenth-century English pamphlets by Gould, Fige, and Ames, but also a history of Hesiod, Horace, Ovid, and Juvenal, as well as the more modern French tradition of La Bruyère, La Rochefoucauld, and Boileau.[3] Lord Rochester uses the tradition as a mode to convey impotence; Samuel Butler twists the reader's expectations of Amazons in his *Hudibras*; Swift seems to copy portions of Ames's *Folly of Love*; Addison translates Semonides' creation story in the *Spectator*; Lady Mary Wortley Montagu, a feminist in her later years, translates Boileau's satire *Contre les femmes*. Each of the poems assumes a knowledge of the tradition, from Oldham's "A Satyr Upon a Woman" (1678) which accuses a deceptive loved one of being "an human image stamped on fiend" to Pope's "Epistle to a Lady," which combines harsh anti-feminism with a richly ambiguous portrait of an ideal woman who combines the best of both sexes.

The context of antifeminist satires creates a myth of as-sumptions that resonate in the satirists' minds. Woman, as violator of the authority of her contractual bonds to the patriarchal order, dares to disdain that authority in the Restoration and early eighteenth century, and the poems examined describe a satiric fiction of that rebellion. Satire, as Robert C. Elliott, Alvin Kernan, Maynard Mack, and others have demonstrated, creates a fiction of power, an illusion or a mask which allows the persona to separate the author from the emotional bond created with his victim.[4] That mask may be one of violence, of anger, of impotence, or of patronage,

so that he may, for a time, create a rhetorical stance which
releases him and like-minded readers from the charms of
woman—and simultaneously absolves him and his readers
from the responsibility for all that he finds reprehensible.
Sometimes the poems are frankly aggressive, even murderous
or blasphemous. At other times, they are recognitions of the
impotence of a narrator forced to confront his own desires as
he assaults female autonomy. But I am also arguing that the
satirist is not always fully in control of his persona, or he
may not, especially in the lesser satires, understand or even
wish to explore the complexities of his relation to the tradition, the conventions, and the myth.[5] In some instances the
antifeminist satiric theme seems to be used to exorcize one
female individual from the mortal world, as in the case of
Oldham, who rhymes a woman dead and curses her with an
eternity of tortures in the seventeenth-century tradition of
the *satyr*. In other poems the entire female sex comes to
embody all that is offensive to the larger society—most frequently as a threat to the patriarchal order. Or sometimes the
antifeminist satires may express an individual satirist's desire
to project whatever is most frightening or unsettling in his
own psyche onto another person. What Michael Seidel writes
of satirists in general seems particularly applicable to antifeminist satirists of the period: the satirist "hopes, almost
prays, that whatever out there threatens him does not by a
stretch of his own imagination absorb him."[6] The female
victim is herself a fiction created to justify the savagery and
the scatology of the tradition. Here I examine some of the
most compelling of the myths: the permissive female or
whore, the powerful Amazon, the learned lady, the ideal
woman, the angel—in order to draw attention to the
commonplaces of the tradition and then to read poems
selected from numerous examples within the classical and
native context.

It is frequently argued that the negative aspects of satire
must be juxtaposed to a positive ideal—that the criticism in
satire implies the hope of something better and that the
satirist's aggressive voice is diffused in an implicit or explicit
norm. Eighteenth-century women, including the scandalous

Laetitia Pilkington, knew well the formula for the ideal woman of the period: she was to be a chaste companion who cheerfully created order and fostered domestic serenity. Such a woman should be even-tempered, patient, modest, and prudent. Addison's *Spectator* No. 15 (17 March 1711) reflects the expectations of the age:

> *Aurelia,* tho' a Woman of Great Quality, delights in the Privacy of a Country Life, and passes away a great part of her Time in her Own Walks and Gardens. Her Husband, who is her Bosom Friend, and Companion in her Solitudes, has been in Love with her ever since he knew her. They both abound with good Sense, consummate Virtue, and a mutual esteem; and are a perpetual Entertainment to one another. Their Family is under so regular an Oeconomy, in its Hours of Devotion and Repast, Employment and Diversion, that it looks like a little Common-Wealth within it self.[7]

It is a woman's natural function to bring stability to the larger society by ordering the domestic world. Scriptural authority for portraying the woman as keeper of family order and enhancer of the larger social order was often cited by both men and women. Even scholar Elizabeth Elstob noted that she aspired to "the Glorious Character of a Virtuous Woman" described in Proverbs 31:13: "She seeks wool and flax, and works with willing hands," though in the same breath Elstob protests that she cannot and will not attain that ideal.[8]

In the fiction of satire, men on the one hand describe women as inherently giddy and unstable, while on the other they create an ideal woman, the mirror of their highest expectations, who is to establish order in the domestic sphere. If women are inherently unstable, how are even the best of them supposed to create a stable center? Even John Bennett, curate of St. Mary's and defender of the natural equality of women, did not understand the contradiction inherent in his argument that what is most charming in women is what men find most threatening to the establishment of stability: "The truth is, that restlessness of sensibility, and that inquietude of imagination, which debar the possibility of great attainments, were providentially designed to compose the very life and essence of their grace. They are the very medium by which they please. If they were constituted to have our *firmness* and our *depth,* they would want their native and their strongest attractions. They would cease to be *women* and they would cease to *charm.*"[9] Women apparently understood that very few of their sex were excepted from universal condemnation, but only at the end of the eighteenth century did Mary Wollstonecraft in *The Vindication of the Rights of Woman* (1792) fully comprehend that such a celebration of a distinguished few required a woman to justify her own virtue, talent, or accomplishment by portraying herself as superior to the natural inclination of the sex, as a triumph of reason over nature.

Satire, even in the seventeenth and eighteenth centuries, cannot be confined to a corrective function, and in elucidating the history of the theme of antifeminism in satires of the Restoration and eighteenth century, I show that satire is not limited to one effect—that satire on the same antifeminist theme may be moral, amoral, or immoral, and that to insist on the moral intent of a satirist to reform his victim is to describe the poem incompletely. Satire may be a bitter wind, painful as well as comic. In order for the satire to have a corrective effect, the satirist must indicate that women's vices do not arise so much from nature as from social and cultural pressures. Once this empathy with the satiric victim is voiced, however, the tragic turns to comic, the ill wind blows more kindly, and the satirist acknowledges that he too may be flawed. And then there is, perhaps, some faint hope of reform. Such a kind wind, however, is also the omen forecasting the end of satires against women in the period. Juvenal, as interpreted by his mid- and late eighteenth-century translators, begins to develop a tear in his eye; the path from the whore to the fallen woman leads to greater understanding of the woman's plight, and a shift in blame from her inherent sexual characteristics to her social plight. George Lillo's dramatic fiction, Millwood, in *The London*

Merchant (1731), is a vicious and immoral conspirator, but Lillo allows her to voice a rousing feminist plea for understanding a woman's situation:

> *Trueman:* "To call thee woman were to wrong the sex, thou devil!"
> *Millwood:* "That imaginary being is an emblem of thy cursed sex collected, a mirror wherein each particular man may see his own likeness and that of all mankind!"[10] [IV.xviii]

Though this book gives passing attention to eighteenth-century novels, essays, conduct books, and sermons, I have not tried to present a comprehensive survey of all satiric literature on women in the period, but rather to provide a significant sampling of the kinds of myths created in the poetry, myths which once recognized can then enhance our reading of the mid- and late eighteenth-century literature that often places women at its moral center. Similarly, it would require another and very different study to trace the history of antifeminist thought in Restoration comedy and domestic tragedy. I have not listened very closely to women's voices in this book, for that too is another endeavor. But especially in the period from 1660 to 1750 the voices of women echo the female absorption of male expectations, sometimes in the most subtle ways, and here we can acknowledge these echoes so that the voices of self-definition and self-affirmation can be distinguished. Those voices are very closely intertwined indeed.

II

Rhyming Women Dead:
Restoration Satires on Women

The period from the Restoration to the mid-eighteenth century in England witnessed a burgeoning of satires against women. This satirical literature reveals a revolutionary reconsideration of the position of women in society and the relationship between the sexes. Lively controversy marks particular periods throughout the century. For example, during the Restoration period Poulain de la Barre's *De l'égalité des deux sexes* (1673), *De l'éducation des dames* (1674), and *De l'excellence des hommes contre l'égalité des sexes* (1675), were translated first as *The Woman as Good as the Man or the Equality of Both Sexes* by A.L. (1677), and later as the Sophia pamphlets in 1739 and 1740.[1] At mid-century the publication of de la Barre in the Sophia pamphlets may have been spurred by Mary Wortley Montagu's defense of the female sex in *The Nonsense of Common Sense*. The Sophia pamphlets, *Women Not Inferior to Man* (1739), *Man Superior to Women* (1739), and *Woman's Superior Excellence over Man* (1740), maintained their popularity in 1751 when they were reprinted as *Beauty's Triumph,* and again in 1780 as *Female Restoration.*

Not long after publication of *Female Restoration,* Reverend Richard Polwhele's satire against Mary Wollstonecraft, *The Unsex'd Females* (1798), sparked what became two decades of feminist debate on the rights of women, indicating that "the woman question" remained interesting to readers. The waves of controversy that broke out throughout the period all begin from the patriarchal assumption of the natural inferiority of women and the inherent superiority of men. The seventeenth century ends with Mary Astell's plea for the establishment of a female monastery where women can be free to study and enjoy female companionship, and the eighteenth century concludes with Mary Wollstonecraft's demand that men release women from the chains of male tyranny and lack of education. Though the issues of the debate vary, the controversy over women's situation persists.

The multifarious social, historical, and economic factors defining the position of women in the period will not be the central topic here, and we cannot know how accurately the satires reflect society. Yet surely the threat to the established order brought about by the Civil War and the Interregnum must have played a significant role in encouraging the eruption of satires against lustful, proud, and inconstant women in the late seventeenth century. Satire seems most likely to be the genre of a social order in shambles; it creates "a sense that things have gone wrong, that society or literature or morals are degenerating, and frequently the satirist shows an order ending or the very edifice of civilization crumbling into ruin," as Earl Miner suggests.[2] Historical studies are just beginning to define the status of women in the period, but certainly women were chipping away at the edges of traditional expectations. That women apparently outnumbered men in England (as a result of emigration to America, men's greater susceptibility to the plague, and the Civil War) must have created conflict between a superior male minority and an inferior female majority. Lawrence Stone notes that the number of marriageable girls at the level of the peerage exceeded that of eligible boys.[3] In 1694, for example, one historian estimated that there were approximately ten men for every thirteen women in London.[4]

Earlier in the century the reign of James I had brought an abrupt end to female learning, and both Cavaliers and Puritans later in the century expressed concern about the disturbing effects of women's learning on the family unit and on society at large.[5] Most educational opportunities for women

in the first half of the seventeenth century were provided by
the church. Much of Bathsua Makin's *An Essay to Revive the
Antient Education of Gentlewomen, in Religion, Manners,
Arts, and Tongues* (London, 1673) defends learning by associating it with virtue. The book derives from the famed Anna
à Schurmann's *De ingenii muliebris ad doctrinam et meliores
litteras aptitudine* (1641), translated into English by C.B.
(1659) as *The Learned Maid; or, Whether a Maid may be a
Scholar.* Following Anna à Schurmann's argument, Mrs.
Makin contends that learning will make women more dutiful
daughters and more loving companions for their husbands.
Though women are "the weaker sex," Makin says, their
mastery of the art of verbal warfare will allow them to use
her *Essay to Revive Education* as "a Weapon in your hands to
defend your selves, whilst you endeavour to polish your
Souls, that you may glorify God, and answer to the end of
your Creation, to be meet helps to your Husbands." She
cautions against misogyny, however, for "A Learned Woman
is thought to be a Comet, that bodes Mischief, when ever it
appears."[6]

Two other reformers, Fénelon, as translated by Dr. George
Hickes, and feminist Mary Astell, influenced late seventeenth-
century and early eighteenth-century thinking on female
education. George Hickes (1642-1715) translated and revised
Fénelon's *Traité de l'éducation des filles* (1687) as *Instruc-
tions for the Education of a Daughter, by the Author of
Telemachus. To Which is Added, A Small Tract of Instruc-
tions for the Conduct of Young Ladies of the Highest Rank*
(1704). In a 1684 sermon Dr. Hickes first proposes female
colleges as an antidote to religious enthusiasm and as a means
to direct undisciplined women to realize their natural abilities. Dr. Hickes protests that education can serve as the hand-
maid, not the enemy, of religion, as it was to the Puritans.
Both Fénelon and Hickes argue against women's equality;
each stresses education as preparation for women's traditional domestic role.[7] Hickes's work, portions of which
Richard Steele would later plagiarize and popularize in his
Ladies Library (1714), encourages women to study reading,
writing, arithmetic, Latin, Greek and Roman histories,

modern languages, and moral philosophy. At the same time Hickes cautions women against displaying their wit, and he emphasizes instead the pious purpose of learning.

But Mary Astell (1666-1739) was by far the most influential of the educational reformers. Born in Newcastle, she moved to London in about 1686 and set forth on a thorough plan to make herself a learned woman in preparation for a fifteen-year career of propagandist pamphleteering in behalf of ladies of class. In 1694 she published her most significant work, *A Serious Proposal to the Ladies for the Advancement of their true and greatest interest* (2nd ed. 1695). Unlike Fénelon and Hickes, Mary Astell believes in women's equality; only the sex's lack of education has made women appear to be unequal. She proposes a unique college for female education as a temporary haven for women preparing to be wives, or even a place of permanent retirement. Mary Astell's most specific and practical innovation is to assert women's economic freedom by offering a Protestant monastery as an alternative to marriage. There women could escape worldly pursuits in favor of philosophy and religion. At one point Princess Anne even promised £10,000 toward the realization of the dream, but upon learning of Bishop Burnet's fear that such a "lay monastery" would be dangerous to the church, Anne withdrew her support. In spite of this radically innovative idea, Mary Astell, like other reformers before her, reasserts the validity of the monarchical privileges of a husband.[8]

Some reformers connected the call for the companionate marriage based on mutual affection with the need for women's education. Daniel Defoe in his *Essay on Projects* (1697) expresses sympathy for women and urges learning in order to make women worthy of male attention: "I have often thought of it as one of the most barbarous customs in the world, considering us a civilized and a Christian country, that we deny advantages of learning to women. We reproach the sex every day with folly and impertinence, while I am confident, had they the advantages of education equal to us, they would be guilty of less than ourselves."[9]

In documenting the revolution in attitudes toward the

individual and the family unit in the Restoration and eighteenth century, Lawrence Stone regards the period as one of "affective individualism," of a developing nuclear family unit, and of greater freedom of choice in a marriage partner.[10] While the enclosure of common fields, the weakening of the guild controls on production, the growth of the market economy, and increased geographical mobility may have enhanced male autonomy and familial unity, it is not clear that these forces created an equally increased freedom for women. Some historians, notably Alice Clark, have argued that capitalist development pushed women out of family and domestic industries and took from them the opportunity to make an economic contribution to the family unit, an opportunity that was not restored until the Industrial Revolution.[11] Women, particularly in the middle class, lost their important role as economic partners with their husbands and were relegated to a frivolous leisure. Women's trade activities such as printing, carpentry, candlemaking, and brewing—open to them in the early seventeenth century— were more and more restricted to men during the Restoration. The monarchical privileges of the husband were maintained, and such a patriarchal family unit required a submissive and deferential wife. Property law required women to remain faithful to their husbands in order to insure smooth transfer of estates from generation to generation and to prevent illegitimate heirs.[12] Husbands assumed responsibility for their wives as they did for property, and laws made it difficult for women to hold land, even if it had been bequeathed to them. Divorce remained extremely difficult to obtain, and in spite of John Milton's arguments that those who did not enjoy each other's companionship ought not be required to remain together, in fact divorce was almost exclusively a male prerogative until the nineteenth century. Controversy about the judicial authority over marriage—ecclesiastical or civil— allowed men to deny their marital obligations. Restoration and early eighteenth-century plays, as well as eighteenth-century novels, dramatize increased conflicts between the romantic inclinations of young lovers and patriarchal fiat.

The effect of Puritanism on the status of English women

defies easy clarification. It both improved the status of the
sex and increased male authority over the family. Certainly it
increased the potential for conflict between the sexes. Puritans questioned the authority of king and state, yet they
substituted the father as the patriarchal authority over
women and children. Some of the most extreme Civil War
sects such as the Ranters proselytized sexual freedom for
both sexes, yet Puritans overwhelmingly insisted on
monogamous relationships and prenuptial chastity. While
Quakers encouraged the autonomy of the individual
conscience, and Quaker Margaret Fell (married to George
Fox) justified women's preaching in print, she also defended
women's subjugation to their husbands in all areas except
matters of conscience, but denied women's inferiority as
based on Eve's original sin.[13] Disgruntled men, however,
accused women in the sects of destroying the family unit,
and they urged women to put down their Bibles for a distaff.
W. Gouge in *Of Domesticall Duties* wrote that "if the fear of
God possess not their hearts, though they be the weaker
vessels, [they] do oft make their husbands plain vassels to
them."[14] At the same time that the Puritans reinforced the
strong familial authority of the father, the Civil Marriage Act
and the political theory which encouraged the individual will
in acts of conscience and education gave rise to considerable
conflict.[15] As Keith Thomas has written, "for the most part,
future feminist movements were to base their arguments less
upon any renewed assertion of woman's spiritual equality
than upon natural right and a denial of any intellectual
difference between the sexes."[16] The pamphlet controversy
which followed the Civil War may very well have arisen in an
attempt to put women back in their pre-Civil War place, to
reestablish their traditional role. Tantalized by the freedom
of conscience and the belief in the equality of the soul in
eternity, women in the Restoration may well have sought
new freedoms on this earth. It was the Puritans, however,
who seemed to foster the titillating uneasiness about sexuality—the self-consciousness about sexual affairs that breeds
fascination with pornography.

While feminist protest occurred a century later in America

than in England, the reevaluation of women's roles apparently began in France before it flourished in England.
Feminist philosophy came to England from Charles I's
French wife Henrietta Maria, from French feminist Protestant schoolmasters who escaped from the Continent, and
from the large number of translations of French romances,
conduct books, satires, and pornography. In a survey of fifty
such bawdy works, Roger Thompson has tentatively found
that a preponderance of writers and readers of pornography
and obscenity in the period derived from the strictest Puritan
backgrounds.[17] A startling number of translations from the
French in the late seventeenth century were explicitly pornographic. Every major pornographic book on the Continent
was known in England within a year. Reprinted in the
original language in England, perhaps made more fascinating
with Italian or French titles, such obscene books as Pietro
Aretino's *Ragionamenti* (1584) and the anonymous *La
Puttana errante* in the manner of Aretino (1660), Ferrante
Pallavicino's *La Retorica delle Puttane* (1642), Nicolas
Chorier's *Satyra Sotadica,* and Jean Barrin's *Venus dans le
cloître, ou la religieuse en chemise* (1683) were sold in
England in popular translations. *L'Ecole des filles* (1655) was
available in England by 1668, for Samuel Pepys writes that
he "stopped at Martins my bookseller, where I saw the
French book which I did think to have had for my wife to
translate, called *L'escholle de Filles*; but when I came to look
into it, it is the most bawdy, lewd book that ever I saw,
rather worse than *putana errante*—so that I was ashamed of
reading in it"—but he bought it, read it in secret "for
information sake," and burned it.[18] The translation published in England, *The School of Venus of the Ladies delight
reduced into rules of practice,* is known to us because the
publishers were indicted in 1688. Legal action against
pornography culminated in the 1725-27 suits against Curll
for publication of *Venus in the Cloyster* (1724). He was
fined and sentenced for "an offence at common law, as it
tends to corrupt the morals of the king's subjects," destroying the peace of the government, "but if it is destructive of
morality in general; if it does, or may affect all the king's

subjects, it then is an offence of a public nature."[19]

The renewed proliferation of pornography in the mid-seventeenth century may well have been part of a larger movement against authority of any kind, a revolt that progressed from religion to politics to sexual mores. David Foxon observes that seventeenth-century pornography centers "on the figure of the permissive female—the whore as against the father."[20] We can account for the fascination and obsession with the whore, as Foxon does, by relating it to the revolt against Puritan repression and the rise of the libertine philosophy, the reliance on the senses rather than on reason, and increased pressures for individual choice. Pornography then may have offered men an escape from responsibility. In addition, however, the whore (and her prototype Eve) came to symbolize man's ambivalence about the female sex. As Simone de Beauvoir has written, throughout the history of literature men have projected their deepest fears about carnality onto women, for women may seduce, dominate, and destroy them.[21] The satiric myth of the whore confirmed male superiority and patriarchal attitudes; men could generalize that unlike men, all women personified lust. If women rather than men were accused of uncontrollable passion, the responsibility for carnality rested on women's provocative shoulders. This myth allowed men to ignore an individual female's feelings and emotions and created an acceptable way to deal with the larger social anxiety created by the loss and shifts of economic, political, and religious authority. The satires reestablished within the poem the myth of men's power over women.

Many of the Restoration satires against women claim that their purpose is moral, their intention is to reform. Of satire in general, John Dryden cites Heinsius's authority in the *Discourse Concerning The Original and Progress of Satire* (1693) when he notes that "Satire is a kind of Poetry, without a Series of Action, invented for the purging of our Minds; in which Humane Vices, Ignorance, and Errors, and all things besides, which are produc'd from them, in every Man, are severely Reprehended."[22] Dryden claims that the positing of an ideal, a positive norm, is an equally important function of satire. Near the end of the seventeenth century such satirists as Thomas Shadwell, Sir Richard Blackmore, and Jeremy Collier justify satire on moral grounds, and call the satirist a physician to an ailing world.[23] As an extended arm of the law, satire also could punish those who offended against those laws or mores which were not easily brought to the attention of a court. Swift suggests in *The Examiner,* No. 38, that the origin of satire may have been such a primitive need to indict wayward members of society:

> I am apt to think, it was to supply such Defects as these, that Satyr was first introduc'd into the World; whereby those whom neither Religion, nor natural Virtue, nor fear of Punishment, were able to keep within the Bounds of their Duty, might be with-held by the Shame of having their Crimes expos'd to open View in the strongest Colours, and themselves rendered odious to Mankind. Perhaps all this may be little regarded by such hardened and abandoned Natures as I have to deal with; but, next to taming or binding a Savage-Animal, the best Service you can do the Neighbourhood, is to give them warning, either to arm themselves, or not to come in its Way.[24]

Some satirists contend that they may in fact inspire real social action which counters the evil exposed in the satire. According to that view the satirist presents a picture of a "just and true society locked in a moral struggle with a false one," as Northrop Frye suggests.[25] The satirist affects, at least, to be a defender of established values; he hopes to act on the mind of the reader in order to create a climate favorable to change. The derisive effect of fine satire may be mitigated "by the moral judgment which is combined with it in one act and one feeling," Louis Bredvold argues. Thus the moral judgment may be "transformed and elevated into indignation, a state of mind of which the judge need not be ashamed."[26] The satirist may pose as a public servant, Robert Elliott writes, for "he is . . . a moral man appalled by the evil he sees around him, and he is forced by his conscience to write satire," to write with Juvenal's *saeva indignatio*.[27]

Satire's purport, then, is to correct through presenting the worst examples, but nearly every satirist at some point expresses some uncertainty about the efficacy of satire. In the mid-eighteenth century, Edward Moore, for example, in *The World*, No. 9, voices a commonplace: "But it is the misfortune of general satire, that few persons will apply it to themselves, while they have the comfort of thinking that it will fit others as well. It is therefore, I am afraid, only furnishing bad people with scandal against their neighbours: for every man flatters himself, that he has the art of playing the fool or knave so very secretly, that, though he sees plainly how all else are employed, no mortal can have the cunning to find out him."[28] Swift, in the person of the hack in *A Tale of a Tub*, questions the reformative power of the satire mode: "Satyr is a sort of Glass, wherein Beholders do generally discover every body's Face but their Own; which is the chief Reason for that kind Reception it meets in the World, and that so very few are offended with it."[29] Even as late as the turn of the eighteenth century, a translator of Juvenal's satires, William Gifford, suggests that while the legitimate object of satire is to scorn the vicious, such an end may not even attract the attention of its satiric object: "To laugh even at fools is superfluous;—if they understand you, they will join in the merriment; but more commonly, they will sit with vacant unconcern, and gaze at their own pictures."[30]

Whether satire leads to reform in the case of satires against women probably cannot be determined, but part of the fiction of satire, the myth created by the work, is that the satiric persona often intends to reform the world. He hopes at least to create an attitude conducive to change. On the other hand, it is entirely possible that some residual belief in the mystical power of the satirist/magician to harm or destroy the victims of his satire (the diametric opposite of the power of satire to reform its victim) informs the antifeminist satires of the period. Robert Elliott has traced this idea to its source in the earliest satires. According to Aristotle's *Poetics*, Old Comedy developed from the improvised

satires of the leaders of Phallic Songs. The Phallic Songs
could be used for comic or tragic purposes, either "the invo-
cation of good influences through the magic potency of the
phallus" (the impulse to reform the victim) or "the expul-
sion of evil influences by means of the magical potency of
abuse."[31] "The word" may itself become a weapon, the song
a phallic instrument of power. The individual attacked may
become ill or even die as a result of the magic potency of the
song. Though the explicit intention of the satirist to wound
or kill his victim is metaphoric rather than literal in seventeenth-century England, the anthropological history of the
Phallic Songs suggests the ritualized nature of the satires and
the function of that ritual in contributing to social unity and
to defense from external attack. The satirist becomes the
spokesman for a group in jeopardy.[32]

In most of the satires included here, the aggressive impulse
seems at least as important as the impulse to reform, and the
particular quality of the genre is its ability to allow the interplay of both impulses in an ambiguous way. The Restoration
satires may be violent and Juvenalian, or more subtle and
Horatian, but the adoption of an aggressive persona, an attacking voice, is persistent. The antifeminist satires follow a
series of conventions: the majority hold no intrinsic interest
for their intellectual concepts or linguistic manipulations, yet
these ritualized and conventionalized structures may have
served social, political, or religious functions. The conventions help create an air of rationality in the midst of angry
accusations, a voice of order in the midst of disorder. Alvin
Kernan has suggested the parallels between aggression and
satire, that "the most elegant method of directing and
managing aggression is ritualization, a process in which aggression is both expressed and channeled by certain rhyth-
mic, formalized, and habitual actions." Satire, he continues,
may be seen as one of the ways "in which man has learned to
control aggression and manage it to useful ends."[33] It is that
management of aggression, of antagonism toward women,
that satires on women seek to shape. Wit, then, helps to put
balm on the wound that that satire has created. Kernan
notes, "The satirist seems always to pretend to praise what he

is in fact blaming, . . . and though we all recognize the game for what it is, know in fact that the blame is intensified by the pretended praise, such irony still seems necessary."[34] Wit simultaneously releases aggression and helps to rein the aggressive impulse. It is my purpose here to catalogue some of those clever and witty devices and *topoi* that repeat themselves throughout the history of misogyny, particularly in the Augustan period.

Aside from the motives of the particular historical moment, there may be within satire an atemporal motive to cope with the satirist's deepest fears through attacking his victim with wordplay. The satirist may be attempting to expel, or at least to project, that portion of his self which he finds most reprehensible. Kernan's second relevant contention is that the very aspects of the genre that are repetitive and dull serve the function of reassuring the audience "that the old dangers are being controlled in the old ways." He adds, "This feeling of reassurance is strengthened by the fact that the images of the myth give a negative value to the illogical and the irrational, to the formless, the meaningless, that which comes from nowhere and goes nowhere."[35] In seventeenth-century satires, women come to embody the very absence of patriarchal order and hierarchy that men most fear. Kernan also identifies a Myth of Satire as "a decaying metropolis in which a tyrant rules a polyglot mob, a countryside of ruins and jungle in which savage animals stalk their prey, and a heaven from which the gods have long departed."[36] Certainly satirists claim to describe the world as it really is, though that too may sometimes be part of the myth of satire, part of the fiction created by an indignant persona.

There is an identifiable fiction of satire against women, a myth to which such satirists subscribe. Women in the myth of satire represent a world of disorder, and the satirists rage at the female power to seduce and overpower them. Women are accused of rebellion against all aspects of patriarchal order and authority. Society easily accepts a satire against the things it most fears, especially if those things are created by the object of the satirist's attack. As that object, women become a metaphor for all that is threatening and offensive to the society at large. Satire, then, helps men to survive their fears, to remain potent when threatened with impotence, both real and imagined. The formalized ritual of the anti-feminist satire within the tradition reassures the threatened male minority. The myth of satires against women includes the myth that women create chaos, and the imposition of form (satire) on formlessness provides meaning and rationality when the fear of meaninglessness and insanity arises.

Even before the seventeenth century, women had traditionally been divided between those who save men's souls and those who damn them. Satire allows for exaggeration and extreme accusations; it is a form which tolerates monsters. Seventeenth-century satires against women rarely offer any alternatives to the fallen women they present; no norm is offered as a relief to the picture of women's depraved condition. In late seventeenth-century England, the cause of man's fall from grace, Eve, and the fictions surrounding the Creation are an important focus of antifeminist satires. As the prototype of all women, Eve, according to the Myth of the Fall, brought chaos into the world with her lust for the forbidden; she caused man's recognition of sexuality, his knowledge of death, and his loss of innocence.[37] All of these dangers become associated with the entire female sex, but especially women's responsibility for men's recognition of their sexuality. The satiric myth defines women by their very nature as whores. Such an association is not, of course, unique to the seventeenth century; medieval misgynist clichés, for example, describe women as lascivious, adulterous, faithless, malevolent, and vain. A number of seventeenth-century satires express similar assumptions, and a study of satires such as John Oldham's "A Satyr Upon a Woman" (1678), the anonymous *Misogynus* (1682) and *The Great Birth of Man* (1686), and Robert Gould's *Love Given O're* (1682), the last with its various satiric responses, reveals examples of conventions of antifeminism in the period—all are satires that make little pretense of reforming the object of their satiric attack.

John Oldham wrote two minor poems which are explicit

in their antifeminism: "A Satyr Upon a Woman, who by her Falshood and Scorn was the Death of his Friend" (1678), and "Upon a Lady, Who by overturning of a Coach, had her Coats behind flung up, and what was then shewn to the View of the Company" (pub. 1683), the latter seldom reprinted because of its pornographic nature. "Upon a Lady," an eleven-stanza poem in awkward tetrameter couplets, criticizes Phillis for unfairly attacking her lover from behind. The poet compares her backside to a lustrous distracting star. The light, bawdy, and rollicking poem is decidedly inferior to Oldham's other antifeminist poem, "A Satyr Upon a Woman."

During the period of time just preceding his writing "A Satyr Upon a Woman," Oldham, son of a dissenting minister, became acquainted with Rochester, Dorset, and Sedley, probably because of the popularity of his "A Satyr Against Vertue," written in July 1676 and published without permission in 1679. Harold F. Brooks lists the poem as appearing in *Satyrs upon The Jesuits . . . and some other Pieces* in 1681, though it is listed in the title as having been written in 1678.[38] Appearing in collected works in 1682, it was judged too obscene to be published in Bonamy Dobrée's reprinting of the 1854 bowdlerized edition by R. Bell. The only nineteenth-century edition was Bell's, and we now await H.F. Brooks's complete edition of the poems.

In "A Satyr Upon a Woman" John Oldham writes in the Elizabethan tradition of Hall, Marston, and Marvell, who, mistakenly believing the word *satire* came from the Greek *satyr*, used harsh and violent techniques in their poems.[39] The poem is not an imitation of Horace, Juvenal, or Boileau, though Oldham writes numerous classical imitations on other subjects. Oldham may have been influenced by his friend Rochester, as well as by Robert Gould, whose works are discussed later in this chapter. Like Gould, Oldham employs violent language, twisted syntax, rough meter, and scatology in his attack on a woman. The couplet rhymes are often strained (seize/skies; blest/chas'd), and sometimes even ignored (breath/forgave). The syntax and meter are no better: "Guilt, which should blackest *Moors* themselves but own, / Would make through all their night new blushes dawn" or "Curses, which may they equal my just hate, / My wich, and her desert, be each so great." in his well-known advertisement to *Some New Pieces* (1681) Oldham indicates that the harsh prosody and tone suit his ends: "And certainly no one that pretends to distinguish the several Colours of Poetry, would expect that *Juvenal,* when he is lashing of Vice and Villainy, should flow so smoothly as *Ovid,* or *Tibullus,* when they are describing Amours and Galantries, and have nothing to disturb and ruffle the evenness of their Stile."[40]

Though we do not know if an historical incident occasioned the poem, Oldham inveighs against a woman "who by her Falshood and Scorn was the Death of his Friend."[41] The fear that women cause the death of men is made explicit; the satirist intends to avenge the death by using the power of the poem to kill her. Addressing the gods who will aid him in throwing the offender into eternal darkness and damnation for her crime, the satirist makes no attempt to reform the woman, for she evades redemption. Fearing that the gods themselves may have joined the perjured, the satirist usurps the function of the gods to become "Witness, Judg, and Executioner":

> Arm'd with dire Satyr, and resentful spite,
> I come to haunt her with the ghosts of Wit.
> My ink unbid starts out, and flies on her,
> Like blood upon some touching murderer:
> And shou'd that fail, rather than want, I wou'd
> Like Hags, to curse her, write in my own blood.[42]

According to the fiction of the poem, the satirist's friend loved the woman, and she turned base and false to that love. It is never made explicit whether she actually murdered him or he died from a broken heart. In any case, the satirist curses her power (and thus all women's power) over men. The lover adored her, and even on his deathbed he worshipped her. The object of love becomes the object of the satirist's hate. In writing the poem, he employs ritual to reassure men that they can retaliate against the power of women to seduce and dominate them.

Oldham focuses on two conventions of satires against women. First, the guilty woman's beauty is "criminal." A daughter of Eve who collaborates with the devil, she seduces men by her attractive exterior. Her paint hides her natural ugliness and deceitfulness. One passage closely parallels Swift's scatological poetry: "Mischief adorn'd with pomp, and smooth disguise, / A painted skin stuff'd full of guile and lyes, / Within a gawdy Case, a nasty Soul, / Like T—— of quality in a gilt Close-stool" (p. 143). Angry because the woman's guilt has not made her ugly, the satirist claims that his curses will destroy her physical beauty. He curses her with the love of the devil, with unrequited love, with the clap, and with an impotent lover. The poem denigrates her to a non-human being, a devil incarnate: "Vile'st of that viler Sex, who damn'd us all!" she is "an human image stampt on fiend."

Worse than her treacherous beauty, however, is her breaking of contractual oaths—with her lover and with her God. Her treachery becomes a metaphor for the hypocrisy of political, religious, and social bonds. She brings to mind Jesuits, town fops, buffoons, and Westminster squires in her perjury: "Less guilt than hers, less breach of Oath, and Word / Has stood aloft, and look'd through Penance-board; / And he that trusts her in a Death-bed-Prayer, / Has Faith to merit, and save any thing, but her" (p. 144). The satirist's bonds with Heaven, he repeatedly stresses, remain intact. The curses he utters are like prayers that heaven will turn to fate. He calls on the larger society to join him in straining to invent some wittier punishment. The satirist's stance is one of engaging the audience in a shared feeling of disgust with a rising chorus of curses. Finally, in a witty turn, he curses her with the retention of her sanity so that she will be fully cognizant of her pain. He wants her sin to become her eternal punishment:

May then (for once I will be kind, and pray,[)]
No madness take her use of Sense away;
But may she in full strength of reason be,
To feel, and understand her misery;
Plagu'd so till she think damning a release,
And humbly pray to go to Hell for ease; [p. 147]

The poem is among the most primitive representatives of antifeminist satires in its violence, which verges on the edge of uncontrolled anger. Only the wit of the satirist keeps the chaos from falling into madness. The ritualized conventions of antifeminist satire stabilize a rhetorical stance which releases and yet contains aggression. As a spokesman for all men who fear women's power to entangle men's emotions, the satirist imagines a fiction of power and assaults the "weaker" sex in a societally sanctioned substitute for physical violence; the satire contains the aggressive impulse, substitutes for it in a ritualized and satisfying way, and speaks powerfully for the most impotent of all—the dead.

Many of the conventions of antifeminist satires appear in "A Satyr Upon a Woman." A liar and a jilt whose painted exterior hides her interior rottenness, the "human image stampt on fiend" possesses no soul. But unlike other antifeminist satiric fictions, "A Satyr Upon a Woman" lacks an address to reprobate women, a presentation of portraits from history, a visit to the underworld, a scene in the boudoir, and a framework with a dissenting adversary. The lady is condemned as a daughter of Eve but without the context of a creation story.

Restoration satirists most frequently trace the "history" of women's pride and lust to its source in Genesis. In loping, awkward verse, *Misogynus: or, A Satyr Upon Women* (1682) tells of woman being created from the dregs: "Whate're was left unfit in the Creation / To make a Toad, after its ugly fashion, / Of scrapings from unfinished Creatures had, / Sure was the body of a Woman made."[43] The satirist fondly recalls a lost age of womanless procreation when Woman so befuddled man that he relinquished his natural asexual state to copulate with the female sex. Man's sexual need for women, then, is woman's fault. He is not to blame if he lusts after woman; she made him do it by assaulting his rational faculties.

Similarly, in *The Great Birth of Man* (1686), woman falls explicitly because of her pride and lust. Created from "a well-spar'd Rib," she brings chaos roaring and crackling into the world when she falls to the serpent's intricate rhetoric:

> Now crak ye Poles, unhinge ye Heav'ns, and shake
> Ye mighty Arches, let the whole World Quake:
> In Sable Clouds, stand still O Sun, and Mourn;
> Let Mountains from their Roots, with Storms be torn.
> The Ocean with its weighty Billows Roar,
> Tumbling in heaps upon the groaning Shoar,
> To see a Prodigy, so vilely great,
> Baffles the Blood'st Birth of Pregnant Fate.[44]

Eve climbs the forbidden tree to seek greedily the largest apple. After Adam's fall, the poem concludes with his advice to all men to beware of women:

> Secure your selves by Countermining Arts,
> Lest they blow up, or else betray your Hearts.
> Take heed, for when, like Crocodiles, their Tears
> Do gently Fall, then's greatest cause of Fears:
> Then their deceitful Hearts design a Prey,
> And in the midst of seeming pity Slay. [p. 23]

In one of the responses to Gould's satire, *Love Given O're*, Richard Ames in *The Folly of Love* (1691) twists the traditional myth of the creation story so that Eve's pregnancy precedes the Fall, and she eats the apple because she has an uncontrollable craving for it:

> Love's solemn Rights not long had been fulfil'd,
> But his new Spouse perceiv'd she was with Child;
> And tho he strove by all kind acts to please,
> Yet all in vain, she could not be at ease,
> Until by stealth to save her longing, she
> Had tasted of the one forbidden Tree: [p. 3]

The anonymous satirist in *On Women* (1698) uses double-entendre to argue that woman is "a cross-grained Creature" who causes a stitch in man's side because he gave up his rib:

> Yet some there are, who in a grateful Mind,
> Would soundly rib their Husbands, cou'd they find
> A good tough Cudgel, and make this their Answer,
> They but restore what *Eve* stole from their Grandsire:
> And His a Reason too (as't hath been try'd)
> A bad Wife sits so close t'her Husband's Side.[45]

So women assist men only in helping them to sorrow, disease, and poverty.

One of the finest verse satires against women which includes a creation story, Robert Gould's *Love Given O're: Or, A Satyr Against the Pride, Lust, and Inconstancy, & c. of Woman* (1682), incited two decades of lively attacks and counterattacks.[46] Gould, a satirist of considerable rank and importance, is consistently omitted from Augustan anthologies, in part because of the harshness of his line in an age of the heroic couplet, and in part because of his obscenities. Born about 1660 and orphaned in early childhood, Gould first served as a domestic in London and later in the employ of James, Earl of Abingdon.[47] His *Poems, Chiefly Consisting of Satyrs and Satyrical Epistles* appeared in 1689, and his other significant works include *A Satyr Against the Playhouse* (written 1685), aimed at Mrs. Barry and Thomas Betterton;[48] *The Satire Against Man* (1689, revised and enlarged 1709); a play called *The Rival Sisters*, based on Shirley's *The Maid's Revenge*; and *Innocence Distress'd*, published posthumously in 1737 by his daughter Hannah.

Gould's references to John Oldham and Lord Rochester indicate that he was fully aware of the recent manifestations of antifeminist verse satire. Rochester's daughter, Lady Anne Baynton, is Gould's "Adorissa," and he acknowledges his poetic debt to Oldham in "To the Memory of Mr. Oldham" (1683) upon his death.[49] Like Oldham, Gould wrote panegyrics to women such as "A Funeral Ecologue to the Pious Memory of the Incomparable Mrs. Wharton" (1685) and to

the "Incomparable Eleanora" in "Mirana, A Funeral Ecologue: Sacred to the Memory of that Excellent Lady,
Eleanora, late Countess of Abingdon" (1691). Like Oldham
too, Gould's poetic treatment presents such women as exceptions to the sex that is otherwise abominable. In praising
Lady Dorothy, wife of Sir James Long of Draycot-Cerne,
Wiltshire, for example, he calls her "a fresh example that
there are wise women beside these two or three mentioned in
scripture."[50] The implied norms against which the women in
the verse satires are judged usually appear in separate poems
in the Restoration. The fiction of the phoenix who is an
exception to her sex or the angel who transcends sexuality
sets a standard against which to judge the horrid ladies of
antifeminist satires, but they are only implied norms which
do not appear within the satires themselves.

Love Given O're and the series of satires it occasioned are
elaborate explorations of the myth of satires against women.
Women are Eve's daughters, dangerous temptresses who
seduce men and lead them to irrationality, immorality, and
even death. Taken together, this series of satires presents
most of the issues of concern to late seventeenth-century
England, and the series is among the finest representatives of
the genre of antifeminist satires and rejoinders. *Love Given
O're*, for example, combines rugged and bawdy language with
classical and medieval conventions to present a skillful transition from the satirist's personal pain to a condemnation of
the sex as a whole. *Love Given O're* is typical of antifeminist
poems in its address to a reprobate woman, its catalogue of
evil women drawn from classical and biblical history, its
creation story and reference to daughters of Eve, its vision of
hell as populated with women, its boudoir scene, its association of women with metaphors of the wind, ships, disease,
and death, and its structural use of the dissenting adversary.
In *Love Given O're* the poet celebrates his newfound freedom
from Silvia's enchaining of him by inciting his muse to
"Gainst the lewd Sex proclaim an endless War." The narrator
begins with the creation story and condemns women for their
"Crab-like Nature," which resulted from the crookedness of
the "fatal Rib." Women envy Eve for the glory of her fall.

Like Eve's apple, women appear alluring, though they, like the apple, possess a dark center of mortal sin. Hints of subsequent satires on women—including Swift's boudoir poems, Pope's "Rape of the Lock" and "Epistle to a Lady"—give the poem further intrinsic interest. *Love Given O're* is as violent as Juvenal's Sixth Satire, and it certainly provided sufficient pretext for other satires and rejoinders.

In iambic pentameter couplets, *Love Given O're* justifies the violence of its satire by woman's unequivocal commitment to pride, lust, and inconstancy. The poet acknowledges that a few women are good, but because of their own concern for morality these women will not be offended by his railing at others of their sex. Unlike Oldham, Gould claims a moral purpose for his satire, and the satire is an analysis of the ways women entice men. In the tradition of Juvenal's Sixth Satire, he strikes out in a diatribe against wives in particular. He cautions men to seek a wench, not a wife, if their "Tyde of Nature boist'rous grow, / And would Rebelliously its Bands o'reflow" (p. 3).[51] Given the example of Silvia, the satirist argues, men should see that woman's word is worthless. Women break personal promises, marriage contracts, and religious vows. Such a fear of women's inconstancy may well represent man's fear of woman's autonomy.[52] Though Gould's poetic voice claims that Silvia is powerless now because he has banished her from his heart, she is powerful enough to intrude on the poem; and he concludes by using her as an example of the most inconstant of women. It is her freedom of choice that he is really attacking.

Gould uses Restoration actresses as examples of lust, women in their boudoirs as examples of pride, and a faithless widow as an example of inconstancy. He proves women's lust with a series of portraits of whores with allusions to Sodom and Gomorrah and to Juvenal's Messalina. From high-placed lustful women he descends to their daughters, the modern actresses Bewley, Cresswold, and Stratford. Bewley's lust was contagious, and she populated hell with the victims of her disease:

Yet, when she found that she could do no more, ⎫
When all her Body was one putrid Sore, ⎬
Studded with Pox, and Ulcers quite all o're; ⎭
Ev'n then, by her delusive treach'rous Wiles,
(Which show'd most specious when they most beguil'd)
Sh'enroll'd more Females in the List of Whore,
Than all the Arts of Man e're did before.
Prest with the pond'rous guilt, at length she fell,
And through the solid Centre sunk to Hell: [p. 4]

The satirist seeks to assuage men's fears that they cannot satisfy women by explaining that women are insatiable by nature, and all women long to be whores. A wench will drain a man dry: "That Whirl-pool Sluce which never knows a Shore, / Ne're can be fill'd so full as to run ore, / For still it gapes, and still cries—room for more!" (p. 3). A woman's vagina resembles the grave, and the inevitable rhyme for "womb" is "tomb." The life-giving part of the anatomy gives women their power to create and their power to kill by causing men to lose their rationality and to sicken and die of venereal disease. Within the satire the womb signifies woman's differentness, her otherness, and her power.

The lust that a whore openly displays to the world vies only with the sordid private orgies of her boudoir. The scene in the lady's dressing room anticipates the association between lovers and lapdogs in Pope's "Rape of the Lock," though Pope's allusions suggest the sexuality of the relationship subtly, while *Love Given O're* exploits it. In "Rape of the Lock," "*Shock,* who thought she slept too long, / Leapt up, and wak'd his Mistress with his Tongue" (I. 115-16). But *Love Given O're* teems with lust:

How, when into their Closets they retire, ⎫
Where flaming Dil—s does inflame desire, ⎬
And gentle Lapd—s feed the am'rous fire: ⎭
Lapd—s! to whom they are more kind and free,
Than they themselves to their own Husbands be. [p. 5]

Issuing a cursory apology to Modesty, the satirist affects to doubt that women understand the virtue, since again "Pride is the Deity they most adore." He resorts to a conventional scene attacking women's artful attempt at the dressing table to delude themselves that they are avoiding their own mortality.

A gay fop interrupts the diatribe to ask the satirist to excuse woman's pride because of her beauty: "Who'd blame the Sun because he shines so bright, / That we can't gaze upon his dazzling light?" The adversary's interruption offers an excuse for the satirist to respond with renewed vigor, this time citing the deception of woman's lovely exterior. Gould successfully employs the formal verse satire convention of an adversary in order to move from woman's pride to her inconstancy. Women are as inconstant as the wind, "wanton Swallows," or a ship tossed on a wave. The poem closes with an unrelenting catalogue of women's vices. The infamous Ephesian matron "made a Brothel of her Husband's Tomb." Even in hell and in death women will make men their dupes. The satirist concludes with a primitive curse: if men insist on marrying after they have heard the satirist's warning, then let them bear all the curses that women can invent. In fact, matrimony is a curse in itself.

Love Given O're, like Oldham's "Satyr Upon a Woman," holds aggressions in check while it uses convention and ritual to vent men's violent feelings toward the women who turn away from them. The curse at the conclusion of Gould's satire is directed as much against men's stupidity in succumbing to women as it is against women themselves. Probably because it is witty and comic at the same time it expresses anger, the poem inspired a satiric paper war between the sexes over the next two decades. The first response to this torrent against women was *The Female Advocate, Or an Answer to a Late Satyr Against the Pride, Lust, and Inconstancy of Women, Really Written by a Lady in Vindication of her Sex* (1686). The initials "S.F." which follow the brief remarks preceding the second edition of 1687 represent Sarah Fige, who asserts that she reluctantly emerges from obscurity because of her contempt for *Love Given O're.*[53]

Twice the length of *Love Given O're*, *The Female Advocate* is not as lively and succinct as its inspiration, but it is worth examining as a prototype of defenses of the sex. Fige senses, and in fact explicitly states, that to suggest that women are superior to men is as antifeminist as arguing that they are inferior. The "blasphemous wretch" who wrote *Love Given O're* has attacked the sex, she argues, because those who love women too much turn into their most vigorous enemies. The female sex should not be universally damned any more than men should be universally praised: "But that Heaven should make a Male and Female, both of the same Species, both indued with the like rational Souls, for two such differing Ends, is the most notorious Principle, and the most unlikely of any that ever was maintain'd by any rational Man." Though she hints that women may seem more pious and devoted than men, it is only because men "neglect that which should make them so." She ingeniously argues that neither sex is innately superior to the other, but the failure of men's moral education makes the male sex *seem* inferior. She contends that men who curse women resemble devils who curse their own self-instigated hell; men unwittingly collude in creating and perpetuating female vice.

Though the poetic meter of the couplets in *The Female Advocate* is sometimes rough, the close reasoning and acute psychological perception in the early sections of the poem counter the attack on women's pride, lust, and inconstancy by saying that the satirist in *Love Given O're* has simply accused women of his own sins. It is Gould, and all men, who deserve eternal punishment, not women who are men's "only steady and most constant bliss." Perhaps, Fige gleefully suggests, the satirist himself loved the notorious actress Bewley. Whatever men say against women should be turned against them: "But to say truest, is to say, that she / Is Good and Vertuous unto that degree / As you pretend she's Bad, and that's beyond / Imagination" (p. 13).

Fige too confronts the question of women as Eve's daughters. She refutes Gould's claim that the devil created Eve, for that would deny God's omnipotence and omniscience. Women, formed from purified matter rather than "dull, senceless Earth," help to perfect man, the incomplete and barren sex. Adam, the representative of all men, bears more guilt for the Fall than Eve since his command came from God and Eve's came from Adam: "She had the strongest Tempter, and least Charge." Those who cavil against the sex because of Eve have forgotten that a woman, the Virgin Mary, bore Christ, and consequently they blaspheme in their antifeminist sentiments. Though Fige seems at times to argue for the superiority of women, she repeatedly returns to the notion that men have neglected their innate potential for piety, goodness, and devotion. Manners, not nature, make men inferior: "Thus have I prov'd Woman's Creation good, / And not inferiour, when right understood, / To that of Man's; for both one Maker had, / Which made all good; then how could *Eve* be bad?" (p. 2). Women are not daughters of Eve, and each woman has her own soul.

> But I'm no *Pythagorean*, to conclude
> One Soul could serve for *Abraham* and *Jude*:
> Or think that Heaven's so bankrupt, or so poor,
> But that each body has one soul or more.
> I do not find our Sex so near ally'd,
> Either in disobedience or in pride,
> Unto the 'bove-nam'd Females (for I'm sure
> They are refin'd, or else were alwaies pure)
> That I must needs conceit their souls the same,
> Tho' I confess there's some that merit blame: [p. 15]

The idea that the male provides movement while the female provides matter, and that the male and female represent the active and passive opposing principles is an Aristotelian argument for female inferiority, a theory derived in part from Pythagorus.[54] In effect, Fige argues against the Aristotelian notion that the female state is a natural deformity, and that women have less soul than men.

Men define women according to their needs, Fige suggests. Men's wives are chaste, and the husbands are the adulterers. When their wives then understandably demand a divorce, how convenient for men to condemn the women and accuse them of their own faults. In fact, Fige heretically contends,

many women would prefer to live single rather than live with
an unfaithful husband or to cohabit without marriage vows:

> Nor do I think there's a necessity
> For all to enter Beds, like *Noah's* Beast
> Into his Ark; I would have some release
> From the dear cares of that same lawful State;
> But I'll not dictate, I'll leave all to Fate. [p. 11]

Having defended women, "S.F." turns in the final (and
weaker) third of the poem to challenge men. Unusual in its
satire against men as a sex, it accuses them of more pride,
ambition, and falsehood than women. They deny their immorality by pretending to catch the pox through the air.
Men seek wives solely to produce heirs to their estates, and
then they neglect their families. Fige provides a catalogue of
such perfidious men, and she concludes with the example
of Brutus, whose treachery proved "that Man more false than
Woman is." The poem concludes with ironic charity:

> I am sorry you do Females hate,
> But rather deem ourselves more fortunate,
> Because I find, when you'r right understood,
> You are at enmity with all that's good,
> And should you love them, I should think they were
> A growing bad, but still keep as you are: [p. 24]

Finally, in a curse much milder than Oldham's or Gould's on
women, Fige damns men to an eternity of hell, while the
female sex, "your imagin'd Fiend, shall live / Bless'd with the
Joys that Heaven can always give."

The Female Advocate combines strength and conviction
with intricate argument. In a specific response to specific
charges, the feminist vents her spleen at Robert Gould,
though without naming him, for associating the entire sex
with evil. Fige thwarts the force of satire against women by
assaulting the assumption that one sex is superior to the
other; she undermines the assumption of patriarchal authority. She insists that men must look to their own motivations
in attacking women, and she also, perceptively, encourages

men to check their "imagin'd Fiend" against the reality of
real women, who, she argues, can withstand the examination.
The force of Fige's rebuttal, as well as her assumption that
the audience understands the issues being debated, suggests
that the charges of pride, lust, and inconstancy continue to
be taken as important issues of debate.

The verse satires on women relating to *Love Given O're*
proliferated in the last decade of the seventeenth century.
The poems follow the general pattern of Gould or Fige,
rabidly antifeminist or stoutly feminist, with minor variations, but the conventions remain much the same. Richard
Ames added his support to the feminist cause with *Sylvia's
Revenge, Or a Satyr Against Man; in Answer to the Satyr
Against Woman* (1688), later reprinted with *Love Given O're*
(1709). *Sylvia's Revenge* has been mistakenly attributed to
Robert Gould, but *The Stationers Register,* 22 May 1688,
indicates it is by Ames.[55] A prolific writer who flourished
from 1691 to 1693, Ames published other satires, including
The Search After Claret (1691), *A Search After Wit* (1691),
and a tragicomedy, *The Siege and Surrender of Mons* (1691).
Sylvia's Revenge, unlike *The Female Advocate,* simply reverses the traditional accusations against women to accuse
men of inconstancy, madness, and bribery. It focuses on
women's need for men to remain constant to them and to be
honest with them. Every species of fop and spark is detailed
as an example of men's inconstancy—the rambling fop, the
squeamish fop, the noisy fop, the cringing fop, the senseless
fop, the city fop. The spark is constant only to his whore,
but husbands bring the worst plagues. A husband's jealousy
causes him to peer proudly into the glass constantly to see if
his cuckold horns have appeared. Not satisfied with pre-
venting his wife from being visited by male companions, the
jealous husband passionately excises male figures from the
tapestry hangings. Any woman who has sense will not marry,
for after marriage her husband will ignore her beauty, wit,
and charm and find a whore more attractive. In retaliation,
women will have to create their own commonwealth where
men will be banished: "Thus when to Hell by Shoals the *Men*
are hurl'd, / *Women* will Reign as Monarchs of the World" (p.

21). Such women will deny their procreative function and will prove their independence from men. The poem concludes with a curse, reversing that in *Love Given O're*, on any woman who seeks a husband: "May she with him spin out a tedious life; / Blest with that much admir'd Title *Wife.*"

Richard Ames later switched loyalties to write the vitriolic attack on women, *The Folly of Love,* but the shift is not as problematic as it might at first seem if we read *Sylvia's Revenge* carefully. The satire on women keeps turning back on itself. For example, in the tradition of past and subsequent antifeminist satires, "The Epistle Dedicatory to those Snarling Currs the Criticks" disavows any specific personal attack on an individual. The female narrator of "The Epistle Dedicatory" affects an apology for her lack of learning which anticipates the language of Swift's poems on women: "Why Gentlemen I hope you'l excuse the want of Learning in a *Woman*; since upon my word I never read *Suetonius* nor *Tranquillus,* for you all know; That a Box of *Marmalade,* Culpeppers *Midwifery,* a Prayer-Book, and two or three Plays, is all the Furniture of a *Womans* Study." Even more pointed is the reference to the ambivalence women are supposed to feel about themselves, probably a projection of the satirist's ambivalence toward the sex. "She" tells the story of Ariadne who, left by Theseus to the wolves and tigers, rose above the curses of men to become "a dreadful Angel," a terrifying symbol of female autonomy who cannot be murdered by men's tongues. The narrator tells of "a Curst Impotence" men have foisted on her. Through the power of their satires, they have taken her voice away:

> *Crocadile* are your tears, Sly silent lyes,
> *Hyaena's* Voice, and *Cockatrices Eyes.*
> *Angels* before you've cheated us and then,
> The cloven-foot peeps out, and you'r all *Divels* ag'en.
> When I my own weak Soul and *Sex* review,
> I hate my self and them as much as You. [p. 7]

The narrator claims she hates herself and the rest of her sex as much as she despises men, the object of her attack. It would be very foreign to the tradition of satires against women to find a counterpart male narrator acknowledging a self-hatred or a hatred of his sex. The ambivalence continues in the female persona's condemnation of an inconstant spark:

> A Vicious constancy he now will own,
> And is not weary of her Service grown;
> While in her Lap, th'inchanted Cocks-comb roks,
> She loveingly requites him with a P—
>   But hold a while m'unwary head-strong Muse,
> In taxing *Men* I my one Sex Accuse.
> The Dart which at the other Sex was thrown,
> Recoils with all its force upon our own: [p. 10]

In general, *Sylvia's Revenge* does not argue for women's superiority or even for women's equality. It focuses on a simple reversal of men's fears that women are inconstant by detailing the inconstancy of every fop in town and warning the female sex against marriage. It argues against men but it does not argue for women.

In 1688 Gould replied to *Sylvia's Revenge* with *The Poetess* and a year later published *A Consolatory Epistle to a Friend Made Unhappy by Marriage*, usually called *A Scourge for Ill Wives*. In 1691 he issued a slightly revised version of *The Poetess* entitled *A Satyrical Epistle to the Female Author of a Poem Called Sylvia's Revenge & c.* In *The Poetess* Milton's patriarchal voice is heard in the inscription from *Paradise Lost*: "Revenge at first, tho' sweet, / Bitter, e'er long, back on it Self recoils." The poetess who wrote *Sylvia's Revenge* (probably Ames) becomes the object of attack rather than Sylvia, and she, like all writing women, is a whore. Gould extends the metaphor of writing and sexuality: a woman cannot be truly witty unless she is chaste; the onset of puberty parallels her urge to write, for writing is like sex; a woman hurling obscenities in print is scratching her scribbling itch: "At Ten Years Age the tingling Itch began / In Streams away thy *Liquid Virgin* ran, / Dissolv'd ev'n but by thinking upon Man" (*Satyrical Epistle*, p. 9).

Forbear thy Scribbling Itch, and Write no more;
When You began 'twas time to give it o'er:
What has this Age produc'd from Female Pens
But an Obsceneness that out-strides the Men's?
Succeeding Times will see the Diff'rence plain,
And wonder at a Style so loose and vain;
And what shou'd make the *Woman* rise so high
In Love of *Vice,* and scorn of *Modesty.*

[*The Poetess,* p. 22]

The extent of a woman's corruption can be measured in her loose and vile language; her style reflects her manners, and her meaning is obscure. Her poetry is as ugly and powerless as her face will be at fifty. *The Poetess,* then, and its revision, *A Satyrical Epistle,* become male weapons aimed at squelching women's creative urges and denigrating those creative urges by making them parallel to lascivious desires. Women's desire to create is unholy and evil, and the male satire against such attempts will "castrate" female satires against men. *The Poetess* is also remarkable because Gould briefly posits an angelic ideal against which we can judge other women—the "matchless" or "chaste" poet Orinda, Katherine Philips (1632-64). In a reversal of Oldham's "human image stampt on fiend," the ideal woman, like love, produces "Something of *Angel* stamp't on *Human*-kind" (p. 24).

Most of the feminist and antifeminist satires we have discussed in the series of responses to Gould's *Love Given O're* make some reference to an antifeminist tradition, but none is as specific in its borrowing as Gould's *A Scourge for Ill Wives.* The poem describes the woes of marriage to a newly married friend who has found a bad wife, and its picture of deformity, ugliness, and lust parallels Juvenal's Sixth Satire. As a genre painting of "one lewd Woman" conducting her day, it also anticipates Swift's "The Journal of a Modern Lady" (1728-29). Worse than Eve, the wife progresses from lawlessness to incest to promiscuousness. The woman makes fools of men by encouraging them to stupify themselves with drink and even to cause their death: "In vain, for she's to

Tyrant Lust a Slave, / Her *barren Womb's* Insatiate as the Grave; / Barren, nor can it well be any other, / She choaks the growth of one Seed by another" (p. 242). In explicit obscene detail, the poet recounts the way men destroy themselves and each other through woman's capacity to destroy their reason:

> No, no, what ever she dictates, we'll do,
> For all is lawful that she prompts us to.
> Let us not then think of a base retreat,
> Or be impos'd on by a holy Cheat;
> She bids us tast of Man, as well as Meat. [p. 243]

She dresses as a man, encourages riot and murder in the streets, and is an angel of death: "Now rotten grown, each pocky symptom shows / She's like to drop in pieces as she goes. / This modest Creature, this *Black-Angel Saint,* / She has install'd her Bosom Confidant" (p. 245).

While *A Scourge for Ill Wives* is violent, ugly, and obscene, it pales beside the anonymous pair of satires, the feminist *The Lost Maidenhead, or Sylvia's Farewell to Love* (1691), and the antifeminist *The Restored Maidenhead* (1691). In the former the "true reasons" for Sylvia's having jilted her lover in *Love Given O're* are clarified: he raped her while she slept. Made powerless while her maidenhead was stolen from her, she refuses to succumb to male power and mounts an extended curse against the sex. Men, who are full of pride, inconstancy, ignorance, lust, and avarice, would pollute and degrade women's ability to give birth, to give suck, and to nurture men:

> Men blame *us* that we *early* learn to sin,
> But how much *sooner* all *their Sex* begin?
> Which Histories describe, who mix'd before
> They came to *Light,* i' the' very Womb they'd *whore.*
> Debauch the *Nurse* as at her *Breast* they lay!
> And like hot *Jove,* on their own *Sisters* prey. [p. 9]

In a lengthy parody of the journal of a modern lady in antifeminist poems, the satirist compiles a scenario of a typical man's life. He spends his school days poring over bawdy books, pursues a strumpet at fifteen, contracts a clap, fathers a child, and seeks whores wherever he can find them from the Inns of Court to the barber's wife. Men, in other words, are insatiable in their pursuit of women as sex objects. The wounded maiden refuses to adopt the passive female role of weeping and suffering; instead, she retaliates by using the pen as a weapon to curse men with impotency, rot, and plague. She will kill men with words:

> *Bolus* on *Bolus* down their Gullets *cramm'd,*
> And *Pills,* as Chain-shot into *Cannon* ramm'd:
> *Physick,* which may of each *ill taste* partake,
> And all the *nauseous Slops* their *Art* can make.
> *Squills, Aloes, Myrrh,* sweet, bitter, salt and sow'r—
> For *t'other* end—a *Glister once an Hour.* [p. 19]

The rejoinder, *The Restored Maidenhead,* claims to be written from the tears and blood of men. It begins with a false premise—for of course a lost maidenhead cannot be restored—and goes on to claim that surely Sylvia wanted to be raped, as did the prototypical rape victims, Helen and Leda: "O Crime, abhorr'd! no sign of discontent; / No least effort the Robbery to prevent; / Surely he stole her with her own consent" (p. 9). All that the satirist promises is that she will not be raped again.

Perhaps because of the reprinting of *Love Given O're* in 1690, the year following produced a furious renewed assault on women, including the pamphlets just discussed as well as Richard Ames's three works, *The Folly of Love, Female Fireships, A Satire Against Whoring,* and the anonymous *Measures of Love.* Also of interest are *Sylvia's Complaint* (1692) and Gould's *Satyr Against Wooing* (1698). Both *Female Fireships* and *Restored Maidenhead* describe women as "she-devils." Like the devil, they are shape-shifters who seem to be angels but reveal themselves to be fiends.

Restored Maidenhead calls women "cockatrices" in a metaphor that became common. The cockatrice, itself a deformed and deadly creature, hatches from a rooster's egg and possesses the power to murder with a glance. The metaphor of the cockatrice seems to embody men's gravest fears—that women are the daughters of men as well as of Eve, that they are a riddle of creation, and that they have the power to inflict death:

> O how th'enchanted heaps of *Gold* decay,
> The pleasure of the *Musick* wears away,
> Or turns to *Yells*; the *Eyes* uncharming grow,
> And firy Red, like Cockatrices glow.
> The *Angel* fades, the *Hag* and *Wife* appears
> All full of hatefull *Wrinkles,* full of Years;
> Nothing of Woman left but *Tongue* and *Tears.* [p. 3]

The satirist judges women and marriage against the ideal of male friendship, and women threaten that precious thing, too, of course. *Female Fireships* offers only one line as a norm against which to judge the hierarchy of whores from pensionary whores to playhouse punks and "cracks."[56] Having warned his friend, gentle Strephon, who is newly arrived in town, against the countless whores, he concedes that Strephon cannot refrain from whoring, but he can moderate his passions with his "charming bride."

Richard Ames, author of *Sylvia's Revenge,* issued one of the lengthiest and best of the responses to Gould when he switched loyalties to write *The Folly of Love* (1691). The iambic tetrameter poem will be discussed further in a later chapter, in relation to a parallel boudoir scene in Swift's "A Beautiful Young Nymph Going to Bed." The general outlines of *The Folly of Love* follow Gould, with an introductory creation story, a rehearsal of women's vices, a survey of women from the lowest whore to ladies of quality, and an interruption from a protesting female advocate. The comic but rapier sharp satire resembles *Love Given O're* in its pervasive obscenity; most remarkable is its final Utopian vision of a womanless land where men can procreate, like trees, without sex with women. In another satire written in response to *The Folly of Love,* Ames praises Stella in the *Pleasures of Love* (1691). Though it purports to be strongly feminist, the poem praises Stella for being unlike her sex in a now familiar turn. A little love poem introduces the longer poem of praise for Stella. In the creation story of *Pleasures of Love,* women are blameless goddesses who were misled by Adam. Women reform and civilize men—they inspire poets, make soldiers fight and merchants sail. Though the poem intends to be feminist, it urges women to adopt the traditional passive and nurturing roles.

Sylvia's Complaint, a second part of Sylvia's Revenge, however, presents a woman who is unusually sensitive to the paradoxes of a woman's plight. She complains about the restrictions of women's sexual desire. A lost maidenhead means that she must choose between starvation and prostitution. Marriage may mean slavery to a jealous husband, while widows are easy targets for lustful men. The female narrator speaks openly to the author who has created her in his imagination while he reads *Hudibras* in a grove of solitude:

> *O*! *could I change my Sex,* but tis in vain,
> To wish my self, or think to be a Man,
> Like that *wild Creature,* I would madly Rove,
> Through all the Fields of *Galantry* and *Love*:
> Heighten the Pleasures of the Day and Night,
> Dissolve in Joys and Surfeit with Delight,
> Not tamely like a *Woman,* wish and pray,
> And sigh my pretious Minutes all away.
> *Woman* a creature one may justly call,
> Natures and Mans and Fortunes Tennis-Ball. [p. 12]

The Restoration satires against women discussed here most often warn men against believing in the conventions of courtly love lyrics or romance. Women are rigidly defined as proud, lustful, and inconstant; the women in the satires are those who damn men's souls rather than those who save them. Women are devils and daughters of Eve, whores who threaten illness and death, women who seduce and destroy, women who confound men's reason. The satires realistically repeat the studied patterns of accusations and metaphors in poem after poem in an apparent attempt to give definition to the disrupted relations between the sexes. The satires frequently remind one single male soul that his plight is not unique—that all men are likely to be jilted or made fools of by women. The satirist reassures the male sex; he employs a rhetorical stance of providing other men with the powerful word to fend off impotence and passivity. The jilt is made into a monster, the whore into a devil. Men's own desires and needs are projected onto the female sex, and women, who express their longing to be equal, independent, and autonomous in their own feminist satires, tell men, even in *men's* dreams, that they are not active and powerful creatures but "Natures and Mans and Fortunes Tennis-Ball." We do not know if *Sylvia's Complaint* was written by a man or a woman, but in a sense it does not matter. The "imagin'd Fiend" in the dream Sylvia reports to a man is a symbol of powerlessness. The fiend, she says, is only a tennis ball. The woman of the poem claims that woman is defined by man, and that definition makes her a plaything in man's game. She claims that it is preferable, in seventeenth-century England, to be a man, and she seems to understand that antifeminist fictions play the game of satirizing women, of hitting the tennis ball, as an aggressive substitute for men's own powerlessness in the face of their social and sexual need for the opposite sex.

III

The Better Women:
The Amazon Myth and *Hudibras*

Feminists and antifeminists alike, those who believed women to be inferior, equal to, or superior to men, all agreed that seventeenth-century women should use whatever talents, virtues, or education they had to support and nurture men. Even those who argued that women were not inferior to men insisted that if women gained some of the knowledge and some of the education of men, they must, nevertheless, remain ladies; when women look like men or act like men, it "unsexes the ladies," a phrase often applied to women who sought education in Restoration or eighteenth-century England. In one of the earliest expressions of this fear, in Ben Jonson's *Epicoene* (1609), the author demonstrated the rampant fever of literary ladies when they recruit others to their "masculine" cause: the ladies "giue entertainment to all the *Wits,* and *Braueries* o' the time, as they call 'hem: crie downe, or vp, or what they like, or dislike in a braine, or a fashion, with most masculine, or rather *hermaphroditicall* authoritie; and, euery day, gaine to their colledge some new probationer."[1] Capable of corrupting other women with her ideas, the learned lady becomes a pervasive metaphor for the unnatural woman who refuses to perform the natural functions of her sex and who actively usurps the functions of the male sex. Such women may form isolated colonies or societies of ruling women, as female philosophers and "princes," who find ingenious methods for overcoming their lack of physical strength. In his much translated feminist defense, *The Woman As Good As the Man,* Poulain de la Barre cites approvingly the example of the Amazons, who demonstrate that even women's supposed physical inferiority is a matter of social conditioning, when he writes, "They that are taken up and employed in painful Exercises, are stronger than *Ladies,* who only handle their Needle, and this may encline us to think, that if both *Sexes* were equally Exercised, the one might acquire as much Vigour as the other; which, in former times, have been seen in a Commonwealth; where Wrestling, and other Exercises, were common to *both*: The same is Reported of the Amazones, in the South Part of America. We ought not call weak men effeminate or strong women, men."[2]

In seventeenth- and eighteenth-century literature the male presentation of powerful and frightening female societies in men's imaginations often focuses on the myth of the Amazon women, who represent, as the "imagined fiend" and the "unsexed lady," women's ability to form a Utopian society in which men are unnecessary for procreation or protection.[3] In the myth of Amazonian societies, the women of necessity evolve a government by and for women because they have been deserted, marooned, or widowed. Women alone discover they do not require men's protection or domination, and they develop their talents at martial arts, especially archery. They dress in military costume to signify the importance of war in the maintenance of their society, even amputating their right breasts in order to improve their marksmanship. The women procreate annually by venturing to their borders to mate with male partners, but without love or passion. In one eighteenth-century version, Samuel Johnson's translation of the Abbé de Guyon's *Dissertation on the Amazons* (*Histoire des Amazones Anciennes et Modernes,* Paris, 1740), virgins were required to kill three men before mating in order to insure that they would not become enamored of the sex.[4] Male offspring born to Amazons were mutilated, killed, or cast off, while young girls were immediately adopted into the female community and trained to hunt. Thus women usurped the authority men once had over their lives, and the function of the male sex was denigrated to an annual sexual servicing.

Amazon societies appear prominently in John Fletcher's *The Sea-Voyage* (1622), Thomas D'Urfey's *A Commonwealth of Women* (1685), William Cartwright's *The Lady Errant* (1635-38), the anonymous *Female Rebellion* (c. 1659), Joseph Weston's *The Amazon Queen* (1667), and Edward Howard's *The Women's Conquest* (1671) and *The Six Days Adventure* (1671).[5] These seventeenth-century plays were not intended to argue for women's right to rule. In the preface to *Six Days Adventure,* Edward Howard writes, "Perhaps it is more the authority of usage and manners, than the law of nature, which does generally incapacitate the Rule of women, there being not seldome to be found as great abilities in them (allowing for the disadvantage they have in not being suitably educated to letters,) as are to be observed in men of greatest comprehensions . . . their characters in this Play being rather made use of to confirm the judgement and practice of the world in rendring them more properly the weaker Sex, than to authorize their government."[6]

The seventeenth-century plays revolving around Amazons frequently create a myth of the masculine woman succumbing to her romantic and sexual desire; her commitment to a band of women or to a political philosophy of self-sufficiency is short-lived. The Amazon community dissolves when love overcomes the women's passion for independence. Their desire to rule pales when juxtaposed to the desire for masculine admiration. Thomas Heywood in *Gunaikeion* (1624) claims that after the lengthy history of the Amazons' victories, they were finally conquered by Alexander the Great, who enthralled Thalestris [Minithra], queen of the Amazons, and she bore his child.[7]

In Thomas D'Urfey's *A Commonwealth of Women,* the prologue draws a parallel between women's forgetfulness of their domestic duties and learning: "For Wit oft draws the Wife to leave her Spouse, / To take a small refreshing at our

House." The Amazon's song of liberty is more a comic and plaintive lament for men's lost love than an impassioned feminist demand for independence:

> Then since, we are doom'd to be Chaste;
> And loving is counted a Crime,
> We'll to our new Pleasures make haste,
> Sing, Revel, and laugh out our Time,
>   And do what we can,
>   Not to think of a Man
> But to make the best use of our Prime.[8]

The women in D'Urfey's commonwealth are not born Amazons. Their hatred of men and their establishment of an Amazonian community occur because French pirates stole their queen's child and husband. Once the royal nuclear family is reunited, all the Amazons seek husbands too. When left to themselves they indulge in sensual fantasies about men.

A Commonwealth of Women and other plays reassure men that when women are left to themselves they will crave men and destroy their own power by quarreling among themselves. The Amazons, as stereotypical silly women, often quibble and dissent and openly avow their desire for men. When two Amazons quarrel over the possession of a man in John Weston's *Amazon Queen,* they settle their disagreement by agreeing to trade him off—each will have him a year at a time. In *The Women's Conquest* by Edward Howard, the women petition for changes in the sexist laws which allow husbands to dispose of their wives by fiat. The Amazons, more militant than in other plays, gain control of the king and take men prisoners. But there is considerable dissension among the women (again, two queens quarrel for possession of one man), and when the king yields to their demands and refuses arbitrary divorces, the ruling Amazon commands the women to give up arms and acknowledge that they cannot fight against love: "and let your conquests henceforth be to love, / And give Men sole supremacy— / I hope our Kingdoms shall unite in making / Laws may fit each Sexes duty."[9] The conclusion expresses the moral for this play, and for most Restoration plays featuring Amazonian societies: "And Women hence from us this pattern take, / Love, and obedience, your best conquests make." Even Amazons have no weapons against love.

Addison provides a similar resolution of the Amazon myth in the *Spectator* No. 434, 18 July 1712. There the annual communion between the two sexes becomes the happy occasion for a congenial gathering. The government of women and the neighboring government of men form a mutual protective league against common enemies. Here is part of Addison's version of the education of the females in the Amazon community:

> The Girls of Quality, from six to twelve Years old, were put to Publick Schools, where they learned to Box and play at Cudgels. . . . They were afterwards taught to ride the great Horse, to Shoot, Dart, or Sling, and listed into several Companies, in order to perfect themselves in Military Exercises. No Woman was to be married till she had killed her Man. The Ladies of Fashion used to play with young Lions instead of Lapdogs. . . . There was never any such thing as a Blush Seen, or a Sigh heard, in the Commonwealth. The Women never dressed but to look terrible, to which end they would sometimes after a Battel paint their Cheeks with the Blood of their Enemies.[10]

But the conclusion to the *Spectator* No. 434 emphasizes the women's weaknesses, for their pregnancies and miscarriages lead the female governing officials to request men's aid in their defense. Having united with the men to defeat a common enemy, the women find themselves debilitated. The *Spectator* continues: "In short, after a few Years of conversing together, the Women had learnt to Smile, and the Men to Ogle, the Women grew Soft, and the Men Lively." Normal sex roles are resumed, and the two nations unite in lasting peace. Again the natural weakness of women, childbearing, interferes with their independent existence. Their requesting the aid of the male sex restores the more "natural" situation of the sexes' attempting to please each other and resolving to live in harmony.

In a still later version, Samuel Johnson as *The Idler* in No. 87 (December 1759) contends that Amazonian activities would prove unappealing to English ladies, but should they wish to dominate men, their own civil wars would undermine their authority. And the Idler dryly concludes with the familiar expectation that women will succumb to love. The old maids "will not easily combine in any plot; and if they should ever agree to retire and fortify themselves in castles or in mountains, the sentinel [the women] will betray the passes in spite, and the garrison will capitulate upon easy terms, if the besiegers [the men] have handsome sword-knots, and are well-supplied with fringe and lace."[11]

Samuel Butler employs the Amazonian myth in his satire *Hudibras* (Part I published in 1663, Part II in 1674, and Part III in 1678) and, in fact, provides a prototype of the Amazonian woman in Trulla, who appears throughout the eighteenth century in literature and art, including Hogarth's series of engravings of *Hudibras*. In a short satire entitled "Women," Butler unflinchingly assaults women's foibles and invents a phrase that is constantly repeated in eighteenth-century satires against the sex—that women, following Aristotle's argument, have no souls at all:

> A Parsons Wife, some Critiques use to Recon
> Half-way in Orders, like a Foemall Deacon
> That by their Husbands Copys, are ordaind,
> And made their Vicars, at the Second Hand;
> And by their Spirituall Callings, have their Shares
> In ordering the Parishes Affairs.
> And chang the Nature of their Sex, betwixt
> The Clergy, and the Layety Commixt.
> The one half of the world have been begot
> Against the other Parts Designe and Plot.
> The Soules of women are so small
> That some believe th'have none at all;
> Or, if they have, like Cripples, still

Th'ave but one Facu[l] ty, the Will;
The other two are quite layd by
To make up one great Tyranny:[12]

In his various thoughts on women written during the course of his life, Butler delights in satirizing women for their naturally timorous nature, their bedevilment of men at the Creation and after, and their personification of the ancient Furies. He reserves violent language for profligate women, yet he stuns us with his perceptions of the similarities between pornography and romance: "There are more Baudy Pictures made of Lucrece, the Martyr of chastity, than ever were of all the Common Prostitutes of all Ages and Nations in the whole world." He defends the double standard, yet he deplores confining virtue in women to a negative quality—to nothing but chastity—"As if that Sex were capable of no other morality, but a mere Negative Continence." Elsewhere he expresses a similar sentiment: "And yett virtue in Women in the ordinary Sence of the world signifies nothing else but Chastity; and vice the Contrary; as if they were Capable of neither good nor Bad above the Middle."[13] Thus we have to tread very carefully in assuming that the satire on "Women" indicates Butler's unequivocal condemnation of the sex as his considered personal view. He argues with equal vehemence for female governance in his random prose observations: "The Governments of women are commonly more Masculine then those of men: For women delight in the Conversation and Practices of men; and men of women. This appeare's by the management of State Affayrs in the Reigns of Queen Elizabeth, Catharine De Medices Regent of France, and the Princes [Princess] of Parma in the Low Cuntrys, compard with the best of any other Christian Princes of those times."[14] At first the passage seems to be a feminist defense of female rulers, but with more precise attention to the language, we see that Butler is using pallid words to restate John Knox's charge in *First Blast of the Trumpet Against the Monstrous Regiment of Women*—that a ruling woman is a "monstre in nature."[15] A female government can only succeed if the women imitate male rules, and yet that means the women are monsters who contradict their nature. According to Knox, women are not natural rulers, though some women may seem to possess wit and reason that is superior to the wit and reason of some men.

Filled with references to the interchangeable nature of sex roles, Butler's long satire presents a foolish Puritan knight, Hudibras, whom women overpower in physical combat, tests of wit, struggles for governance, and the use of the romantic conventions of love. Hudibras is the dupe of the belligerent warrior Trulla, the unfaithful wife (who is called both a whore and an Amazon), and the learned and crafty Widow. Earl Miner has argued that "the advocacy of female superiority by Butler is so extraordinary and so persistent in the poem that it must be considered a central theme."[16] While I agree that sex roles and sexual ambiguity are central to *Hudibras,* I do not think the poem is, finally, feminist, for Butler's persona seems to argue that women, in order to be superior, must be something other than themselves—Amazons, goddesses, angels, or masculine rulers.

Trulla, who overpowers Hudibras physically, makes her first appearance among the bear-baiters in Part I. In love with Magnano, the tinker, she stands beside him in battle. "A bold *Virago,* stout and tall / As *Joan* of *France* or *English Mall.*" She puts aside her modesty, runs "a-tilt at men," and demonstrates that government by women may bring "pernicious consequence" to men.[17] Butler makes her an enthusiastic warrior. When a reconciliation between the debating Ralph and Hudibras seems imminent, Trulla revives the fight. She charges Hudibras from behind in an imitation of the manner in which Hudibras planned to take the Lady: "He that gets her by heart must say her / The back-way, like a Witche's prayer" (I.iii.343-44). Trulla is a triumphant victor: "With home-made thrust the heavy swing, / She laid him flat upon his side, / And mounting on his trunk astride, / Quoth she, I told thee what would come / Of all thy vapouring, base Scum" (I.iii.852-56). Trulla then uses her female power to manipulate men and to turn the law (in this case military law) against them. As a governing power the belligerent Trulla arranges for Hudibras to take the place of the imprisoned character Crowdero. Butler thus suggests that the only pernicious consequence women like Trulla bring to government is a justice unfavorable to fools. In a satiric reversal of our expectation that men possess reason, Butler makes reason feminine, and yet women, as the agents of rationality, create strife among men.[18] When Trulla conquers Hudibras she demeans him by requiring him to wear her mantle. They metaphorically trade sex—she becoming the powerful male, he the defeated female.

Women use their sexual power to make foolish men weak and feminine, just as Trulla employs her physical power. Butler reverses the romance conventions of the heroic male and the passive female to make the female heroic and the male a captive of his own stupidity. Love, Hudibras argues, makes men into the conventional females, passive servants:

> 'Twas he, that brought upon his knees
> The *Hect'ring* Kill-Cow *Hercules*;
> Reduc'd his *Leager-lions* skin
> T'a *Petticoat,* and made him spin:
> Seiz'd on his *Club,* and made it dwindle
> T'a feeble *Distaff,* and a *Spindle.* [II.i.351-56]

Hudibras maintains that when women marry men without loving them, it is the equivalent of rape: "A *Rape,* that is the more inhumane, / For being acted by a *Woman.* / Why are you *fair,* but to entice us / To *love* you, that you may despise us?" (II.i.327-30).

Similarly, the unfaithful wife of the Skimmington procession (a public mockery of an adulterous wife and her cuckolded husband) creates domestic strife, usurps her husband's authority, and makes her defeated husband feminine.[19] The "*Amazon* triumphant" is preceded by her petticoat hung high as a banner:

> Bestrid her *Beast,* and on the *Rump* on't
> Sate *Face* to *Tayl,* and *Bum* to *Bum,*
> The *Warrier* whilome overcome;
> Arm'd with a *Spindle* and a *Distaff,*

> Which as he rod, she made him twist off;
> And when he loyter'd, o're her shoulder,
> Chastiz'd the *Reformado* Souldier. [II.ii.641-48]

Hudibras, whose view we know is suspect, sees the victorious show as pagan and anti-Christian; and after some mild disagreement from Ralph, they agree that the only just occasion for public mockery is when the husband has retreated without concern for his honor:

> But to turn *Tayl,* or run away,
> And without blows give up the Day;
> Or to surrender e're the *Assault,*
> That's no mans fortune but his fault:
> And renders men of *Honor* less,
> Then all th'*Adversity* of Success.
> And only unto such, this Shew
> Of *Horns* and *Petticoats* is due. [II.ii.723-30]

But as Hudibras works himself into a frenzy of battle against the procession, he defends the female sex against scandal:

> *Women,* that were our first *Apostles,*
> Without whose aid w'had all been lost else,
> *Women,* that left no stone unturn'd,
> In which the *Cause* might by concern'd:
> From *Ladies* down to *Oyster-wenches,*
> Labour'd like *Pioners* in Trenches [II.ii.805-06]

A flying egg interrupts Hudibras's defense of the sex, and the procession turns into a brawl. Hudibras and Ralph retreat—the very act they have most condemned—but they defend their behavior as a bold adventure in the *"Sexe's honor,"* which ought to impress the widow Hudibras is trying to woo.

Hudibras, then, is not idealizing women. Hudibras, who defends the sex in spite of the treachery of the Skimmington whore, sees the procession as an expedient way to woo the Widow. He employs feminism in the cause of romance. In the *Heroical Epistle* addressed to the Lady, Hudibras cites the tradition of the Romans taking the chaste Sabine women by force to prove that men have a right to any woman. It is natural for men to rape women, he argues, and consequently natural for men to exert power over their wives:

> For Women first were made for Men,
> Not Men for them.—It follows then,
> That Men have right to every one,
> And they no freedom of their own:
> And therefore Men have pow'r to chuse,
> But they no Charter to refuse: [*Heroical Epistle,* 273-78]

The entire *Heroical Epistle* assaults the sex and asserts masculine supremacy, though Hudibras finally denies, of course, that his words have specific application to the Widow. The satire unveils the antifeminist logic of such men as Hudibras, Ralph, and Sidrophel, and the reader begins to believe that they deserve to be ruled, fooled, and even tortured by the tyrannical beings, women. In contrast to the greedy and beastly male sex, women use the art and wit men lack to gain power, while men cower in fear. The rule of women, while not to be desired, seems to be more acceptable than the rule of a Hudibras, Ralph, or Sidrophel.[20]

The generally accepted Puritan view was that women are not equipped to exercise political authority, but there are occasional God-ordained exceptions. Though the genuine views of Calvin and "the Geneva group" were quite complex, the Anglicans believed that they argued against government by women without exception, and the Calvinists were often labeled antifeminists. The antifeminist aspects of Puritans in popular lore must have led Butler to allow those implications to be at play in the antifeminist sentiments voiced by Presbyterian Hudibras and Independent Ralph.

The Widow demonstrates the enormous power of women in a variety of ways, but female power exists because men fail to grasp the intricacies of romance conventions. Butler grants women power, but he mocks the conditions under which that power is established and perpetuated. The shrew and Trulla are, after all, whores who understand more about power than the men. To provoke love in men, to make men love them, affords them authority. The Widow demands plain-speaking, something Hudibras cannot sustain for long. She demystifies and deromanticizes love with her wise and cynical eye. She reports, for example, that in addition to romance, love also creates bestial perversions such as Pasiphaie's love for a bull and Semiramis' passion for horses. She persuasively argues that romantic love is not associated with marriage. Marriage is unnatural, an exchange of sex roles between men and women.

In the strongly feminist *The Ladies Answer to the Knight* the widowed Lady mocks Hudibras's *Heroical Epistle* and wittily reasserts the power of women over men.[21] She takes up her pen as a learned writing lady who fulfills men's greatest fears by encouraging domestic discord. Simultaneously she represents that feared Amazon, the unruly ruling woman who ought to be subject to romantic wooing but who refuses to succumb to male romantic subterfuge. She satirizes the defeat of Hudibras's "sword" by Trulla, and reminds him that in breaking his vow to the Lady he has acted in the way women are accused of acting. She exposes his desire for her money, and then uses antifeminist texts to insist on female power: "For if you all were *Solomons,* / And *Wise* and *Great* as he was once, / You'l find Th'are able to subdue, / (*As they did him*) and baffle you" (*Ladies Answer,* 195-98). Because men are attracted by artifice (ruby red lips, eyes like diamonds), she continues, men force women to create more artifice, to pretend to perfection and grace. Women were first made for men, she concedes, but then, in an inversion of the Fall, Mary, a woman, restored men to life: "Since all the *Priviledge* you *Boast,* / And Falsly *usurp'd,* or *vainly lost*: / Is now our Right, to *whose Creation,* / You ow your *Happy Restoration*" (*Ladies Answer,* 249-52).

The Widow calls on men to acknowledge that women rule everything and that any power men believe they have is an illusion. The marketplace, public meetings, the seas, the home, and posterity all fall under women's rule. Every church, every country, every war is women's province:

We Manage things of Greatest weight,
In all the world's *Affairs of State.*
Are Ministers in War, and Peace,
That sway *all Nations* how we Please,
We rule *all Churches,* and *their Flocks,*
Heretical, and Orthodox. [295-300]

The voice of the Lady is so sure, so wise, so strong, that the reader easily accepts her voice as the satirist's, and we share her desire to deflate Hudibras's rhetoric and to expose his arrogance. But Samuel Butler is suspicious of extremes, no matter how righteous his proponent of excess may seem. In his "Thoughts Upon Various Subjects," Butler writes, "The greatest Drunkards are the worst Judges of Wine—the most Insatiable Leachers the most Ignorant Cricks in Women, and the Greediest Appetites, of the best Cookery of Meats—for Those that use *Excess* in any Thing never understand the Truth of it, which always lies in *the Mean.*"[22] The Widow's excessive claims typify, of course, men's most irrational fantasies. If men are distressed with this status, she concludes, let them give place and submit; or if they must, let them seize the unjust power: "Let Men usurp Th'unjust Dominion, / As if they were *the Better Women*" (*Ladies Answer,* 381-82). *The Ladies Answer* attacks conventional attitudes as displayed in heroic poetry. The Lady turns away from domestic duties and from the male sex. She refuses the natural functions of a woman, and she usurps male prerogatives. She refuses to fall in love and to succumb to men's power. Truly an unruly monster who terrorizes men and mocks them, she becomes a satiric fiction of the woman who does not need men.

Hudibras relies on debate rather than action, and each canto and section of the poem fails to reach resolution. The ambiguity in the poem contributes to the sense that the battle for power between the sexes will also remain unresolved. Clearly *Hudibras* indicates that the rule of women, while superior to that of men, is not much to be preferred. The myth of the Amazon—the ruling woman or the mascu-

linized woman who exemplifies man's fear of uselessness—is
defused by creating the counter romantic fiction that love
will lead independent women to relinquish their autonomous
state. *Hudibras* plays with those expectations and turns them
upside down. Butler exuberantly challenges the assumptions
of the myth of the Amazon and forces the reader to reread
antifeminist texts. Butler's Widow refuses to come into the
domestic fold, to acknowledge her inferiority, or to support
and nurture men; with powerful irony, she challenges men to
dare to prove they are as capable as ruling women. Such
women who refuse to exist solely for and through men give
the lie to the romantic expectation that they must solicit
masculine approval in order to give meaning to their lives.
Butler successfully demystifies the autonomous woman, gives
her a rational (if strident) voice, and allows her to mock the
Puritan sects who feared her threat to patriarchal authority.
The frightful female monster, the Amazon, would resurface
to haunt men's imaginations throughout the eighteenth
century and beyond.

IV

"That Lost Thing, Love":
Women and Impotence
in Rochester's Poetry

Butler's *Hudibras* depicts powerful women who attain that power by aping men, and women who refuse to perform the traditional functions of the sex. Like Butler's satire, the poems of John Wilmot, Second Earl of Rochester, mock men's romantic idealizations as much as they mock the sex itself. Rochester never attacks the whole female sex in a poem like Oldham's "Satyr Upon a Woman," but in several of his poems that concern women (notably "Fair Chloris," "The Imperfect Enjoyment," "Timon," and "A Letter from Artemisia to Chloe"), Rochester blames women for the vacuous and ambiguous relationships between the sexes. These satires seem more comic, more witty than the popular diatribes against women, and Rochester frequently maintains that tone by creating considerable distance between the poem's narrator and the women who inhabit the text. Women in Rochester's poems exemplify the satiric myth of the Amazon in their ability to be autonomous, to inspire love, to cause men to lose control; but more than Butler's Trulla and the Lady, Rochester's women remind men of an unattainable ideal of love and womanhood. Love is both the culprit and the longed-for ideal: to love a woman is to fear her power. But Rochester does not seem to pose alternatives to love or to set forth any satiric norm against which we can

judge women or the love of them. The satires, lacking in resolution, create a very temporary illusion of power, and instead
of becoming forceful weapons against the sex (as in the case
of the popular satires), they are monuments to the impotence
of a narrator who is forced to confront his desires.

Rochester wrote to his friend Henry Savile (1642-87) on
22 June 1674 that "I have seriously considered one thinge,
that of the three buisnisses of this Age, Woemen, Polliticks &
drinking, the last is the only exercise att wch. you & I have
nott prouv'd our selves Errant fumblers, if you have the
vanity to thinke otherwise, when wee meete next lett us
appeale to freinds of both sexes & as they shall determine,
live & dye sheere drunkards, or intire lovers; for as we mingle
the matter, it is hard to say wch. is the most tiresome
creature, the loving drunkard or the drunken lover."[1] The
confidence to his friend is, of course, the casual statement of
a libertine philosophy, but it also emphasizes the libertine's
sense of powerlessness, his apparent lack of control over his
"buisniss." Rochester as poet and satirist reveals his recurring
sense of powerlessness in a world of uncertainty. As Carole
Fabricant has written, "Rochester's portrayal of impotence
implies that it is not so much the temporary result of particular circumstances as the inevitable condition of all human
existence: a comprehensive metaphor of man's failure to
realize his desires in the mortal world."[2]

Rochester mocks both those who seek the ideal of loving
relationships between the sexes, and those who have relinquished the possibility of love in this world. Rochester often
makes unconventional use of the conventions of the love
lyric or the antifeminist satire (such as the dream vision, the
aging coquette, the *memento mori*) as part of his assault on
our expectations.[3] In his love lyrics and later satires, Rochester seems to invent new "rules of love" while he undermines
the very possibility of romantic love and romantic conventions. For example, in "Upon Leaving His Mistress" the poet
claims that to insist on the constancy of his mistress would
damn her rather than praise her. He affects to praise his
mistress for being a fecund whore who services an entire
nation. The poet mocks the reader's expectation that to call

her a nurturant mother earth will be a compliment, when he
makes her "universal influence" obscene and lustful:

> See, the kind seed-receiving earth
> To every grain affords a birth.
> On her no showers unwelcome fall;
> Her willing womb retains 'em all.
>> And shall my Celia be confined?
>> No! Live up to thy mighty mind,
>> And be the mistress of mankind.[4] [ll. 15-21]

Further, some of what is treated as unique to Rochester
consistently appears in misogynist satires, Cavalier love lyrics,
or Restoration comedy. For example, some critics have cited
Rochester's association of the vagina with eating metaphors
and its image of an enormous, insatiable cavern as possible
evidence of Rochester's castration fear; but such metaphors
are quite commonplace in late seventeenth-century satires.[5]

Women's beauty, the object of praise according to
romance conventions, may paradoxically cause men to be
damned in Rochester's poetry. The poet in "On the Women
About Town" pleads, "Make the women more modest, more
sound, or less fair!" The whores may doom man to "The loss
of his heart and the fall of his nose." Similarly prostitute Sue
Willis becomes the object of attack because she so readily
enslaves men in "On Mrs. Willis": "Against the charms our
ballacks have / How weak all human skill is, / Since they can
make a man a slave / To such a bitch as Willis!" (ll. 1-4). The
libertine narrator of various songs alternately attempts to
extricate himself from women's power and to deny that their
power exists. He denigrates women as "the silliest part of
God's creation" (l. 4) in the song "Love a woman? You're an
ass!" Woman ranks at the lowest level of society as the un-
worthy companion to fools and wits. The libertine prefers
almost anything to a lowly lady: "Then give me health,
wealth, mirth, and wine, / And, if busy love entrenches, /
There's a sweet, soft page of mine / Does the trick worth
forty wenches" (ll. 13-16).

On the other hand, woman's seeming autonomy merits

violent curses in an earlier poem, "A Ramble in St. James's Park." The narrator enters the crowded satiric scene of St. James's Park, "this all-sin-sheltering grove," to relieve his drunkenness with lechery, "To cool my head and fire my heart," but he becomes a voyeur who observes Corinna's ability to attract every man who passes. The divine Corinna drops to earth because she scorns a god, and the narrator curses her enticingly divine appearance: "But mark what creatures women are: / How infinitely vile, when fair!" (ll. 41-42). He is appalled at her welcoming the advances of three amorous knights, and he berates her with a scatological curse. The divine goddess is reduced to "the savory scent of salt-swoln cunt." He curses himself as well: "Gods! that a thing admired by me / Should fall to so much infamy" (ll. 89-90). He would have preferred that her going with the three knights had resulted from the lust he had aroused in her:

> There's something generous in mere lust.
> But to turn damned abandoned jade
> When neither head nor tail persuade;
> To be a whore in understanding
> A passive pot for fools to spend in! [ll. 98-102]

The narrator then solicits pity by playing the role of a scorned lover who has long suffered the promiscuous activities of his mistress. He is, in fact, angered because she is not, even in some perverse way, faithful to him. Now he curses her ability to dissolve his powers of reason and subject *him* to the mindless powers of love. She is all lust, he all love. In the remainder of the poem the narrator seeks unrelieved revenge with a curse on her womb which parallels the narrator's curse on his useless penis in "The Imperfect Enjoyment":

> May stinking vapors choke your womb
> Such as the men you dote upon!
> May your depravèd appetite,
> That could in whiffling fools delight,

Beget such frenzies in your mind
You may go mad for the north wind. [ll. 133-38]

The scorned lover, the narrator, will reserve his most vitriolic revenge for her until after she is married. He will make her feel his misery by making her spouse jealous, by making her "chew the cud of misery / And know she owes it all to me" as he tears her away from her husband in the very act of sex. Rochester is using the conventional curse against the sex as the conventional retribution of a lover scorned. He returns her scorn, using his power "To plague this woman and undo her." As in Oldham's "Satyr Upon a Woman" (written about five years later), the object of love becomes the object of the satirist's hate. The satirist is hurt that Corinna does not return his love, and he expresses the hurt through anger rather than weeping. The satirist sees himself as sexually impotent when faced with Corinna's lack of feeling, and the only power remaining to him is that of the pen. Chaos will reign before he ceases his attempt to contain her:

Crab-louse, inspired with grace divine,
From earthly cod to heaven shall climb;
Physicians shall believe in Jesus,
And disobedience cease to please us,
Ere I desist with all my power
To plague this woman and undo her. [ll. 147-52]

Rochester turns the conventional curse against the sex to condemn Corinna's lack of feeling. While Oldham, Gould, Ames, and countless other satirists attack women for their lust and inconstancy, the libertine narrator here inverts the reader's expectation and condemns Corinna's resistance to emotion and her resistance to loving him, but he masks his pain with angry curses. Rochester parodies the pastoral model and the Cavalier love lyric;[6] he also elaborates on the standard antifeminist curse and condemns Corinna for her disinterest in him as much as for her lust.

"Fair Chloris in a Pigsty Lay," one of Rochester's early

songs, also appears to be an antifeminist poem. It mocks the idealized shepherdess, Chloris, and the pastoral tradition which created her. The lovely nymph with "snowy arms" and "ivory pails" sleeps against a background of the "murmuring gruntlings" of her pig herd. "Fair Chloris" mocks the reader's expectations, pastoral conventions, the idealization of women, and the illusions of men who seek power over them. Rochester does not provide an explicit norm against which the reader can balance his attitudes toward Chloris, and in that way the poem ends without resolution. The originality of the poem rests in part in its balance of comic and serious elements—the concept of pigs' gruntlings as complaints of the scorching day; the passionate, even sensual, devotion Chloris apparently feels for her pigs; and the swain's plot to rape her which inspires her fear. The poem avoids the celebratory resolution of comedy, though it is filled with comic elements; it skirts the dissolution into chaos that the dark vision of apocalyptic satire would require. Only Chloris, who mastur-bates to ease the excitement inspired by the dream, is satis-fied, and the reader feels the uneasiness of having been tricked, the uneasiness of irresolution. While it is true that Chloris "has it both ways, so satisfying our 'Fair Chloris' and our 'pigsty' expectations,"[7] the reader may catch himself sharing the antifeminist sentiment, and wishing, perhaps with Chloris, that the rape had taken place.

Rochester allows the reader to believe he is a voyeur, unobserved in his vicarious excitement, and then turns the poem to give power to the supposedly passive "Fair Chloris." Very much in the manner of minor Restoration boudoir poems, the poem allows the reader to intrude on a woman's secret and perverse rituals. Rochester allows interplay be-tween the reader's pastoral expectations, turned sensual, and the hidden power of Chloris. In the first stanza it seems Chloris guards the pigs, but we learn that the grunts inspire her sleep. She dreams of gently tending the pigs, but she also has the power to capture a swain:

> She dreamt whilst she with careful pains
> Her snowy arms employed

> In ivory pails to fill out grains,
> One of her love-convicted swains
> Thus hasting to her cried: [ll. 6-10]

The present tense of Chloris's dream makes it seem even more immediate. The swain runs to tell her that her "bosom pig" hangs in danger at Flora's cave, and Chloris's preference for the pig rather than the swain makes her the object of mockery.

Stanza six creates an abrupt turn in the reader's attitude. The swain becomes the villain as the story of the endangered pig is revealed to be a plot against Chloris's honor. The "love-convicted swain" turns into "the lustful slave" as he throws himself on her at the entrance to the cave. Transforming the pigs' groans into the erotic sounds of rape, she awakes fearing that she has lost her virginity. But Nature intrudes to release her, and she realizes she has dreamed. Through masturbation she is restored to the same fair innocent Chloris who lay sleeping in stanza one:

> Frighted she wakes, and waking frigs,
>   Nature thus kindly eased
> In dreams raised by her murmuring pigs
> And her own thumb between her legs,
> She's innocent and pleased. [ll. 36-40]

The reader remains the voyeur—he sees that in her most secret dreams she does desire the swain she has denied. Rochester suggests that Chloris's innocence is not legitimate, and that she shares the mindless morality of her pigs. But she still retains the appearance of power, for the poet seems resentful that a woman can satisfy herself without a man and still remain innocent.[8]

The dream vision of the virgin is, of course, a convention Pope employed most successfully in the eighteenth-century work "The Rape of the Lock." On the day of Belinda's rape, her guardian Ariel conjures up a vision of a beautiful youth who whispers the gentle warning that men may seek to steal her honor. She awakens still innocent, but there is a somewhat muted suggestion that the dream arouses her. The beau's words "ev'n in Slumber caus'd her Cheek to glow" (I.24), and her lapdog, a surrogate lover, awakens her: "when *Shock,* who thought she slept too long, / Leapt up, and wak'd his Mistress with his Tongue" (I.115-16).[9]

Dream visions in minor antifeminist satires of the period frequently recall Eve's fall from innocence, which was brought about by Satan's disguised urgings, and thus such visions become a metaphor for the Fall of mankind. For example, the anonymous "The Maiden's Dream" (1705) describes a virgin's vision as wish fulfillment, though it ends with the maiden being less satisfied than Chloris:

> Once slumb'ring as I lay within my Bed,
> No Creature with me, but my Maidenhead,
> Methought a Gallant came, (as Gallants they can do
> Much with Young Ladies, and with old ones too)
> He woo'd, he Su'd, at length he sped,
> Marry'd methought we were, and went to Bed.
> He turn'd to me, got up, with that I squeak'd,
> Blush'd, and cry'd oh? and so awak'd.
> It wou'd have vex'd a Saint, my Flesh did burn,
> To be so near, and miss so good a Turn.
> Oh! cruel Dream, why did you thus deceive me,
> To shew me Heaven, and then, in Hell, to leave me?[10]

"Fair Chloris" creates extraordinary sensuality in a woman's masturbation by making the reader a voyeur. The poem concludes with the contraries still fluctuating. What Anne Righter says of "The Earl of Rochester's Conference with a Post Boy" may be extended to "Fair Chloris": "It manages simultaneously to magnify and deflate *both* its subject and the orthodox values by which that subject is judged, to invite belief and to undercut it."[11] In "Fair Chloris" we are invited to feel relieved that the rape was only a vain imagining and that her virginity has been preserved. The romantic belief that she remains innocent is also mocked, for Chloris attains sexual satisfaction without succumbing to a man's sexual power. Chloris, like Corinna in "A Ramble in

St. James's Park," remains untouched by man within the present moment of the poem. Chloris and Corinna are observed from afar by the reader and the narrator, but the narrator's distance allows an illusion of control over the women. At the same time the narrator bemoans his lack of power to insist that Corinna love him, to rape Chloris, and even to consummate sex with his mistress in "The Imperfect Enjoyment." One sees why women should be kept at such distance in "The Imperfect Enjoyment," for their very touch causes the narrator to lose control, to subjugate reason to love. Disdain or even pain may paradoxically inflame the passions rather than deaden the feeling. The language of love and death may be exaggerated, both to evoke an ambiguous response to the narrator and apparently to animate love. In another poem, "The Discovery," a man in love may escape his feelings of impotence through the double entendre of "dying":

> But Love has carefully contrived for me
> The last perfection of misery,
> For to my state those hopes of common peace
> Which death affords to every wretch, must cease:
> My worst of fates attends me in my grave
> Since, dying, I must be no more your slave. [ll. 31-36]

In "The Imperfect Enjoyment" the frustrated male narrator directs his satire against his own impotent organ rather than against the mistress. The genre of "the imperfect enjoyment" apparently originated in Ovid's *Amores* II.iii and Petronius's *Satyricon,* chapters 128-40; the Latin, French, and English sources for the poem have been thoroughly documented in recent years.[12] In both Ovid and Petronius the lover finds himself unable to perform for his mistress at the crucial moment. In Ovid the incident is made comic; in Petronius humiliation makes the lover consider castrating himself as punishment for his own inadequacy. The genre reached new popularity in seventeenth-century France and England, and apparently Rochester knew several modern versions. The Restoration examples of the genre vary in how comic they are, who and what is to blame for the impotency, and the kind of curse on the offending organ.

The only action in Rochester's "The Imperfect Enjoyment" takes place in lines 1-18. "Both equally inspired with eager fire," the pair initially share in the foreplay. The woman actively urges consummation, she charms him, and the lover seeks to control his sexual response with his "thoughts":

> With arms, legs, lips close clinging to embrace,
> She clips me to her breast, and sucks me to her face.
> Her nimble tongue, Love's lesser lightning, played
> Within my mouth, and to my thoughts conveyed
> Swift orders that I should prepare to throw
> The all-dissolving thunderbolt below. [ll. 5-10]

He responds to her activity by ejaculating prematurely, and he suffers because he has failed her. She clearly causes his sexual excitement, but she is not blamed for the missed mutual gratification: "A touch from any part of her had done't: / Her hand, her foot, her very look's a cunt."

From this point the poem becomes somewhat static—that is, more satiric than comic, as the language of the poetry imitates the action. Its static nature increases as verbs turn to adjectives, and the distance between the lover's expectations and the reality of his experience increases. He finally despairs: "Trembling, confused, despairing, limber, dry, / A wishing, weak, unmoving lump I lie." At first the self and the organ are synomymous, the penis equated with the soul, and they remain identical for another attempt at satisfaction. But once the speaker acknowledges the futility of renewed attempts, he completely dissociates himself from his penis. The organ takes on a separate identity as the speaker sadly recalls its past days of glory. Called back to the present, the lover launches a violent curse against himself, and he addresses the penis as if it were a detached soldier deserting his military duty.

A central question in reading "The Imperfect Enjoyment" concerns the cause of the lover's impotence and just what

Rochester is suggesting about it. Richard E. Quaintance, citing sources in Montaigne's *Essais* and poems by Remy Belleau and Mathurin Regnier, suggests that in following his sources, Rochester distrusts "the interference of rational or imaginative faculties in a situation properly physical only."[13] Dustin Griffin contests the idea of the mind as a cause of impotence since "indeed, the culprit is the unruly member which is imagined to have a will of its own. It is the offending organ, not the meddling mind, that is cursed."[14] I agree that the lover's "thoughts" aid rather than impede the lover. Beyond that, the cause of the premature ejaculation, it seems to me, is quite clearly the touch of the mistress. The language of the first eighteen lines of the poem confines the cause of the ejaculation to the mistress's touch. "Love" inspires the lover "with eager fire," and the mistress's tongue, "Love's lesser lightning," brings about an ejaculation. The lover can maintain his potency only at a distance; the female's proximity threatens his power to perform, to be manly.

The lady too attributes the failure to love and rapture, not to thought or reason, but she gently chides him as she distinguishes between the love she has experienced and the pleasure she has been denied: "All this to love and rapture's due; / Must we not pay a debt to pleasure too?" But premature ejaculation is followed by impotence: "Eager desires confound my first intent, / Succeeding shame does more success prevent, / And rage at last confirms me impotent" (ll. 28-30).[15] The eager desires exist in the present moment of impotence and "confound" the earlier failure. His *desire* is to swive, and the emotions of shame and rage further complicate that desire. Not surprisingly, her hand which caused the premature ejaculation cannot also relieve his impotence. Love inspired his first attempt to swive, and "love's lesser lightning" first inspired his thunderbolt. As the lover turns to the past, a time of pleasure and power, he creates greater dissociation between past success and present failure, between the self and his sex; he disgustedly curses the offending organ and fashions a metaphor. The self is a prince, the penis a warrior in his behalf who turns cowardly:

Thou treacherous, base deserter of my flame,
False to my passion, fatal to my fame,
Through what mistaken magic dost thou prove
So true to lewdness, so untrue to love? [ll. 46-49]
. . . .
But when great Love the onset does command,
Base recreant to thy prince, thou dar'st not stand.
Worst part of me, and henceforth hated most,
Through all the town a common fucking post,
On whom each whore relieves her tingling cunt
As hogs on gates do rub themselves and grunt. [ll. 60-65]

The separation from the self is very complex, for the request
is for disease or illness to ravage the penis. Love now becomes
the culprit.[16] Love created the erection, caused the premature ejaculation, and perpetuated the impotence. Once
again Rochester mocks the lost ideal of love. Love creates
rapture; it also creates destructive despair.

Two other recent readings of the poem deserve attention.
Carole Fabricant argues that no clear reason for the lover's
impotence emerges, and thus impotence seems "funda-
mentally inexplicable and uncontrollable, an inevitable fact
of life liable to appear at any moment without warning and
without particular reason."[17] Her reading of the poem then is
apocalyptic and tragic, a "vision of impotence and decay."
Yet it seems more likely that the exaggeration of the curse,
while consistent with tradition, adds comic elements to the
lover's self-destruction, though the world of the imperfect
enjoyment is not that uncertain. Rochester cites the touch of
the lady, the lover's rage and shame, and love itself as sources
for sexual failure. Nor can I agree when Reba Wilcoxon says
that the lover "acknowledges an obligation beyond the mere
satisfaction of self and an obligation to the needs and desires
of another."[18] Certainly the mistress is not cursed or de-
graded with other whorish members of her sex, but the
lover's overwhelming preoccupation is with his own lack of
ability to perform, not with relieving his mistress's frustration. Remembered only in the final line, "The wronged
Corinna" becomes merely the spoils of battle to be thrown to

the potent and victorious: "And may ten thousand abler pricks agree / To do the wronged Corinna right for thee" (ll. 71-72). The balance of power shifts from the mistress to warriors who are more virile in the cause of love. The poem resists an antifeminist interpretation, for the lover flagellates himself rather than his mistress.

"Timon," on the other hand, seems to derive its portrait of a faded coquette from the antifeminist tradition. An imitation of Boileau's Third Satire (1674), "Timon" has the superannuated coquette, comic in her attempt to attract young wits, at its center. When confronted by an adversary who inquires about his debauched appearance at the beginning of the poem, Timon presents himself as feeling passive, even impotent, within the world of fools and knaves. Timon seems to identify himself with a coquettish whore, one who knowingly attracts a spark with her affected modesty, but he cynically criticizes himself for succumbing to the distasteful alliance with the sot who invites him to dinner: "I tell him I'm engaged, but as a whore / With modesty enslaves her spark the more, / The longer I denied, the more he pressed. / At last I e'en consent to be his guest" (ll. 9-12). Though the sot is ostensibly less powerful than he, Timon finds himself in the coach of the sot, who tries to assign libelous poetry to him and who leads him to his home to join Halfwit, Huff, Kickum, and Dingboy at dinner. Timon repeatedly claims he is impotent, even when confronted with less powerful companions than he; and perhaps he is impotent in the face of the convention that demands that he politely accept his host's hospitality: "I saw my error, but 'twas now too late: / No means nor hopes appear of a retreat" (ll. 41-42).

The host's wife, Rochester's successful addition to Boileau's Third Satire, perversely embodies woman's ability to inspire love and create impotence. The antiquated coquette who nostalgically yearns for her more youthful past insists on dominating the conversation with her false affectation of learning. Rochester's treatment of the lady is somewhat ambiguous. He emphasizes her sexual desire and her inability to satisfy men's desires.[19] But because Timon, who describes her, is much flawed as a character, we cannot assume that the satiric narrator was without sympathy for an aged woman's plight, even though she appears to be the object of satire in the poem.

Timon introduces the wife as one thing more that must be tolerated at the fool's dinner. A female grotesque, she longs to talk of a lost Cavalier ideal of love, an ideal supposedly attainable in her youth. In the exclusive company of men, she holds forth on the woeful state of poetry and the state of love. No one contests her will, for what she says does not matter. Timon's attitude toward her is clear—as a decayed reminder of lost ideals and lost love, she is a vacuous freak to be endured, comic in her desire to arouse a spark from the men gathered for dinner. Occasional glimmers of her pathetic plight allow for hints of sympathy, however:

> She has been fair,
> Fit to give love and to prevent despair,
> But age, beauty's incurable disease,
> Had left her more desire than power to please.
> As cocks will strike although their spurs be gone,
> She with her old blear eyes to smite begun.
> Though nothing else, she in despite of time
> Preserved the affectation of her prime: [ll. 47-54]

Having lost her sexual power over men, she attempts coquetry, only to remain a faded reminder of her personal past and the past of poetry. She is pitiful rather than frightening, wistful rather than violent in her obsession with love:

> She asked Huff if love's flame he never felt;
> He answered bluntly, "Do you think I'm gelt?"
> She at his plainness smiled, then turned to me:
> "Love in young minds precedes ev'n poetry:
> You to that passion can no stranger be,
> But wits are given to inconstancy." [ll. 61-66]

The host, like his wife, exhibits "more desire than power to please" Timon's palate when the dinner, described in anal and venereal terms, interrupts the portrait and the conversation. Timon associates the piece of beef with a prostitute's arse, carrots with dildoes, the table with "Cullen's bushel cunt." The dinner suggests the loss of pleasure in ordinary experiences of the senses. The lady resumes her plea for a return to the past:

> My lady, she
> Complained our love was coarse, our poetry
> Unfit for modest ears, small whores and players
> Were of our harebrained youth the only cares,
> Who were too wild for any virtuous league,
> Too rotten to consummate the intrigue.
> Falkland she praised, and Suckling's easy pen,
> And seemed to taste their former parts again.
> Mine host drinks to the best in Christendom,
> And decently my lady quits the room. [ll. 101-10]

The lady, by romanticizing love and seeking to recreate perfect romantic love, becomes the object of satire as a representative of society as well as of her sex. Like her husband the host, she fails to provide pleasure; she hypocritically affects to provide a moral standard, yet her only "decent" act is to leave the room. We feel momentary sympathy for the host's wife, who longs for the simplicity and finality of Cavalier love poetry, though Rochester's satiric voice quickly retreats to express Timon's cynicism: the persona flees from the decay of pleasure as well as from the ideal of love. Timon remains the skeptic and libertine, the detached observer who satirizes host, wife, dinner, and fops, but who provides nothing more sensually satisfying in their place.

Rochester's verse epistle "A Letter from Artemisia in the Town to Chloe in the Country" continues the lament for "that lost thing, love." Artemisia, like the host's wife in "Timon," reminds her correspondent Chloe of a past heroic ideal. The ideal and the loss of that ideal interplay in Artemisia's elegy to love:

> Love, the most generous passion of the mind,
> The softest refuge innocence can find,

The safe director of unguided youth,
Fraught with kind wishes, and secured by truth;
That cordial drop heaven in our cup has thrown
To make the nauseous draught of life go down; [ll. 40-45]

The poem presents three variations on the relations between the sexes—Artemisia's, the fine lady's, and Corinna's.
Each contrasts the present state of relationships between men
and women with ideal relationships. Though each attempts to
gain sovereignty through language and manipulation, each
describes the frustration of that attempt in a world of impotence, a world in which the senses can deceive. The poem
begins with Artemisia's protest and immediately establishes
the felt competition between the sexes. If men of wit who
aim at "large returns of praise" cannot achieve their desires,
how can women writers hope to compete? Yet there is something slightly perverse in the exaggeration of the disparity
between the sexes. Artemisia's grave advice to herself to
avoid being a poetess is equally ambivalent: while cautioning
herself that "poetry's a snare," she continues to weave out
the poem. She stresses the gap between the writer's expectations and the reader's perceptions as she addresses herself:

Dear Artemisia, poetry's a snare;
Bedlam has many mansions, have a care.
Your muse diverts you, makes the reader sad:
You fancy you're inspired; he thinks you mad.
Consider, too, 'twill be discreetly done
To make yourself the fiddle of the town,
To find th' ill-humored pleasure at their need,
Cursed if you fail, and scorned though you succeed!
Thus, like an arrant woman as I am,
No sooner well convinced writing's a shame,
That whore is scarce a more reproachful name
Than poetess—   [ll. 16-27]

But she takes lascivious pleasure in violating the conventions
of the town: "Pleased with the contradiction and the sin"
(l. 30). In a world of distorted perceptions the muse inspires

her to delight in the supposed *sin* of writing. Again we en-
counter the notoriety of female poets in the parallel between
wit and whorishness.[20] The equation between whore and
female wit remained a commonplace in satires against
women. William Walsh's Misogynes in *A Dialogue Concerning Women* (1691) would argue against women's learning: "Do not you think Learning and Politicks become a
Woman as ill as riding astride?" And Robert Gould took his
inspiration from Rochester for *A Satyrical Epistle to the
Author of Sylvia's Revenge* (1691):

> Hast thou not heard what *Rochester* declares?
> That Man of Men, for who with him compares,
> Must be what e're the Graces can bestow
> Upon their chiefest Favourite below:
> He tells thee, *Whore's the like Reproachful Name,*
> As *Poetress*—the luckless Twins of Shame. [p.19]

Male wits are also chided for their affinity for whores. It is,
however, not a characteristic of their sex that the wits are
thought to be fools.

In addition to being a *memento mori* of lost ideals, Artemisia is very much a woman of this world who exercises the
skill to articulate the failings of "this lewd town."[21] As the
narrator, Artemisia loosely unifies her letter, a tale within a
tale, with the theme of perceptions misguided and set askew.
Everyone in London shares the state of fools to some extent,
"the perfect joy of being well deceived." Love, once an ideal,
is now distorted in the unnatural worlds of trade, power,
politics, and fashion. Women, fools, and fops deceive others,
but mostly they deceive themselves. There is constant reference to senses deceived: women are "deaf to nature's rule,
or love's advice, / Forsake the pleasure to pursue the vice."
Accurate perception, "clear knowledge," comes from reason's "glaring light," and women perversely avoid it at all
costs. The country bumpkin falls in love with Corinna's
appearance, deceptive as it is, only to have her poison him.
The fine lady mistreats her sycophantic husband in a perversion of conjugal love. Grotesque in her frantic haste, she

bows to a "dirty chattering monster" of a monkey instead of the lady of the house. He represents a surrogate husband, an inversion of marriage.

Artemisia, then, reports to her country friend Chloe about a London which violates nature's rules. Love, supposed to be a joy, has become "an arrant trade." Artemisia wonders, when the fine lady pauses in her elegy to the monkey, "what nature meant / When this mixed thing into the world she sent." The natural way contrasts with man's artful machinations in a passage which seems indicative of some of the most pervasive ideas in Rochester's poetry:

> Nature's as lame in making a true fop
> As a philosopher; the very top
> And dignity of folly we attain
> By studious search, a labor of the brain,
> By observation, counsel, and deep thought:
> God never made a coxcomb worth a groat.
> We owe that name to industry and arts:
> An eminent fool must be a fool of parts. [ll. 154-61]

Just what, then, can be discerned in the poem about Rochester's attitudes toward women? The answer rests in part in Rochester's attitude toward the speaker, Artemisia, for she provides a perspective for us on the fine lady and on Corinna. Critic John Harold Wilson has flatly stated that Rochester was "a raging anti-feminist." He maintains that for Rochester, "The moral is clear; poor, weak, silly woman is capable of incredible monstrosities. Only the man of wit can escape her ravenings."[22] He finds Artemisia unsatisfactory as a norm because of her confusion, hypocrisy, gossip-mongering, and inability to compete with prevailing norms for women. None of these is a convincing argument, however, for Artemisia seems more self-aware than some would allow her to be. Her contradictions resemble a knowing irony more than a blundering inability to cope with the lewd town.[23] More convincing than Wilson is Dustin Griffin, who recognizes that Artemisia "is herself qualified and satirized by herself and by the reader,"[24] but finally we are not certain if she is a satirist or a gossip. Artemisia recognizes what is—a world of women who defeat themselves by misusing their power, a world of perceptions turned askew, a world of fops and fools who invite exploitation, a world in which happiness is not to be found. Artemisia's message is that any apparent triumph— whether of poetry, of love, of wit, of fops, of whores, or of women in general—must be reexamined by an eye capable of perceiving irony and deception, an eye like Artemisia's, however limited her vision may be. Antifeminism, then, is one powerful mode for expressing male impotence as Rochester's poems ridicule those who hope for that lost ideal, love.

Rochester follows the antifeminist traditions we have described with the inclusion of familiar conventions, such as the superannuated coquette, the writing whore, the *memento mori,* and the virgin's dream vision. The satires assume woman's lust, inconstancy, and vanity; they curse her fecundity, her sexual appetite, and her ability to disrupt men's expectations and illusions, while a simultaneous impulse describes her sexual autonomy and power. The satires deplore women's attractiveness and their ability to feminize men even as they lament men's self-hatred and emasculation. At the same time that the satirist narrator wallows in the satiric myth of impotence as a lover, however, the force of his words creates a potent weapon. The satires bemoan the narrator's lack of power while they attempt to establish power through language. The satirist longs for release from his desire, yet he clings to his need for passion. The satirist loves, yet he hates himself for loving and his mistress for inspiring that love. The popular satires of the Restoration transfer the responsibility for love to woman, and more and more to the sex as a whole, as an abstraction that can be attacked without so much reference to the male's own feelings of love. In Rochester's poems, however, the satires on women seem less a means to contain aggression than a means to contain men's pain and vulnerability, and in addition, to gain power through wit and language in the articulation of that pain. Women are satirized for their "killing pleasure" ("A Song," 1685)—their capacity to seduce, dominate, and destroy—but their worst offence, as they are characterized in Rochester's poems, is their unwillingness to love the men who love them.

The poems document the conflicts inherent in experiencing love and sex when the rules have changed and the players, particularly the women, have refused to adopt their familiar roles. If pornography is the reflection of women as men want to affect them, but know they cannot, it is, to some extent, an instrument well suited to the impotent. The rhetorical stance Rochester adopts seems to suggest that he writes from the same impulse as the less artful seventeenth-century pamphleteers. Yet because the narrator allows the reader to recognize that very impulse from which the satires arise, he sometimes frees the reader to share the comic and witty lament for what once defined the relationships between passionate men and women, "that lost thing, love."

V

Rara Avis in Terris:
Translations of Juvenal's
Sixth Satire

Most of the antifeminist satiric stereotypes of women—
including the whore, the coquette, the Amazon, and the
memento mori—appear in the most sweeping of classical antifeminist satires, Juvenal's Sixth Satire on women. Centuries
earlier than Rochester, Juvenal had taken as his subject the
unmitigated depravity of Roman women. Like Rochester,
Juvenal expressed longing for a past ideal age, condemned
the ideal of love, and assumed that lust was the bond between men and women. In Juvenal's Sixth Satire the satirist
bemoans the demise of chastity and longs for a return to the
Golden Age when wives were different: "When Reeds and
Leaves, and Hides of Beasts were spread / By Mountain Hus-
wifes for their homely bed, / And Mossy Pillows rais'd, for
the rude Husband's head."[1] Juvenal's satire is an unrelieved
diatribe against Roman women placed in the frame of advice
to a young friend, Posthumous, who is advised against
marriage. The satire makes no pretense of reforming women,
and yet, unlike later seventeenth-century English satires, it
does not aim to murder women through curses. The end of
the satire seems to be to persuade men who are stricken by
love's darts that they can extricate themselves from the
entrapment of marriage if they will only rid themselves of
illusions about women. Juvenal's central theme is Roman

woman's tragedy—her loss of the essence of womanhood and the substitution of maliciousness and corruption.[2]

The translations of Juvenal's Sixth Satire on woman from Holyday and Stapylton in the seventeenth century to Gifford and Hodgson in the early nineteenth century allow us to see the varying interpretations of one antifeminist text, Juvenal's own Latin version. The most significant version for the eighteenth century was John Dryden's translation of Juvenal's satires, including the Sixth, published in 1692.[3] When Dryden contributed the adulatory preface to William Walsh's *Dialogue Concerning Women* two years before he translated Juvenal, he paid high compliments to Walsh for his learned argument between the woman-hating "Misogynes" and the woman-loving "Philogynes." Dryden's public face in that preface was one of generosity to the ladies, and he aligns himself with the feminist side in the debate over women's equality, dissociates himself from antifeminism, and suggests with Philogynes that "The Dispute is not whether there have been any Ill Women in the world, but whether there are not more Good. For my own part, who have always been their [women's] Servant, and have never drawn my Pen against them, I had rather see some of them prais'd extraordinarily, than any of them suffer by detraction: And that in this Age, and at this time particularly, wherein I find more Heroines than Heroes."[4] Similarly, in Dryden's preface to his translation of the Sixth Satire, he dissociates himself from Juvenal and argues that he did not wish to translate the poem because he found its excessive anger so offensive. Suggesting that the satirist's voice is Juvenal's and not that of a persona, he asserts that the poem "is a bitter invective against the fair Sex," and assumes that women had offended Juvenal the man in some unknown way. He searches for Juvenal's intention, and he determines that it cannot be a moral one.[5] Dryden seems to be asking: If Juvenal condemns the entire sex, what does he posit as a substitute for women in men's sexual and social lives? To avoid the sex would be to end the species, and to warn men of women's artifice acknowledges "that they have more wit than Men: which turns the Satyr upon us, and particularly upon the Poet; who thereby makes a Complement, where he meant a Libel." As a justification for translating the satire, Dryden claims it is not very effective anyway—Juvenal undermines his own purpose. Finally, Dryden rather lamely excuses his translating the satire by indicating that no one else, including Sir Charles Sedley, was willing to translate so violent and obscene a poem, in spite of his pleadings, and that his translation will be harmless because it lacks persuasive power. But he then undercuts the force of these excuses with his own irony: "Whatever his *Roman* Ladies were, the *English* are free from all his Imputations." The argument of the satire, Dryden contends, is "in no way relating to them [Englishwomen]." In this way Dryden takes his place beside all those earlier and contemporaneous satirists who affect to separate their own views from the views expressed in the work. And there is further ambiguity concerning Dryden's views on women when he notes that the Roman women loved "to speak *Greek* (which was then the Fashionable Tongue, as *French* is now with us)." He concludes that "if we will take the word of our malicious Author; Bad Women are the general standing Rule; and the Good, but some few Exceptions to it."

Dryden's translation, like Juvenal's original poem, establishes a narrator who raves misogynistically because he has been scorned. The satire is so extreme, so exaggerated, however, that it sometimes creates considerable distance between the reader and the satiric voice. In the argument, Dryden maintains that he translates the satire precisely *because* it lacks persuasive power. Some more recent critics of Juvenal agree that the satirist's voice is almost hysterically irrational and suggest that his delight in describing the drunken and sadistic orgies of whoring women indicates that he intentionally undermined his own apparent antifeminism.[6] It is unlikely that Juvenal's meaning is ironic, though it is difficult to know; Dryden, at least, claims that the extreme accusations weaken rather than strengthen the force of the satire.

Dryden may not have wanted to translate the Sixth Satire, but he does it superbly well—so well that it is difficult to believe his claims of dissociation. While he may have made it into a dispassionate exercise in translation, several aspects of the translation, when compared to the original work and to the other Restoration and eighteenth-century translations, suggest that Dryden's sly wit is indeed turned against English-women. To the early eighteenth century, Juvenal's Sixth Satire was *the* original antifeminist satire, and Dryden's translation was most frequently cited. The version known to the eighteenth century included very specific sexual detail— Juvenal updated to include Englishwomen's French affectations, references to the mall, park, and theatre, and numerous generalizations about the characteristics of the sex. The significant theme to which Dryden and Juvenal repeatedly return is women's refusal to succumb to the social, legal, and sexual strictures of marriage because of increasing foreign influences, mercantilism, luxury, and excessive leisure, characteristics of Rome and of Restoration England.

Juvenal's explicit obscenity and scatology also find considerable imitation in the late seventeenth-century satires on women. Juvenal's meaning is always clear in Dryden's translation, and Dryden does not omit references to excretion, regurgitation, and intercourse. Apparently he at one time wrote a number of obscene couplets that were not included in the printed text. W.B. Carnochan discovered the seventeen additional bawdy verses on the recto of the back endpaper in a Huntington Library copy of a first edition of the poems of Juvenal and Persius. The editors of the California edition of Juvenal's Sixth Satire have elected to relegate the obscenities to the footnotes in establishing a definitive text, and just why Dryden chose to omit the lines, assuming that it was he who wrote them, is not completely clear.[7] In Messalina's portrait, for example, Dryden omits Juvenal's specific references to her nipples, belly, and engorged sexual parts, but his language still manages to ooze with seamy sexuality:

> Prepar'd for fight, expectingly she lies,
> With heaving Breasts, and with desiring Eyes:
> Still as one drops, another takes his place,
> And baffled still succeeds to like disgrace. [ll. 176-79]
>
> . . . .

All Filth without and all a Fire within,
Tir'd with the Toyl, unsated with the Sin.
Old *Caesar's* Bed the modest Matron seeks;
The steam of Lamps still hanging on her Cheeks
In Ropy Smut; thus foul, and thus bedight,
She brings him back the Product of the Night. [ll. 184-89]

Similarly, specific portraits of Tulla, Laufella, and Ogulnia exemplify female lust in passages that explicitly describe an orgy.

In Dryden's version women's corruption extends beyond the private, beyond the public, to the spiritual realm. Nothing remains sacred. As the poem progresses, women's power over men increases. Women debilitate men—from singers to actors—and they are extreme in their demands. A gluttonous hostess vomits in front of her guests and her husband dares not speak; a learned wife "breaks her Husband's Head"; the Gawdy Gossip's husband gets stuck in the glue of her deteriorating makeup; Bellona's priests are obvious eunuchs. Bellonna's herd of geldings becomes a symbol of the power of women and the impotence of men: "Weak in their Limbs, but in Devotion strong, / On their bare Hands and Feet they crawl along; / A whole Fields length, the Laughter of the Throng" (ll. 677-79). Such a picture of unmitigated corruption is bound to arouse a cry of injustice to women in most rational readers. The convention of formal verse satire, the dissenting adversary, allows for that outcry within the original poem and in Dryden's translation. The young man contemplating marriage queries the satirist:

But is none worthy to be made a Wife   ⎫
In all this Town? Suppose her free from strife, ⎬
Rich, Fair, and Fruitful: of Unblemish'd Life: ⎭
Chaste as the *Sabines,* whose prevailing Charms
Dismiss'd their Husbands; and their Brothers Arms.
                                    [ll. 233-37]

The young man proposes the hypothesis of a *"rara avis,"* a black swan. But the poet responds cynically that such a paragon would constantly boast of her beauty, nobility, and chastity, and that she would be an offensive mate:

> Upbraided with the Virtues she displays,
> Sev'n Hours in Twelve, you loathe the Wife you Praise.
> Some Faults, tho small, intolerable grow:
> For what so Nauseous and Affected too,
> As those that think they due Perfection want. [ll. 262-66]

Even the black swan, the hypothetical ideal woman, is appallingly unappealing; the implication is that perhaps the entire sex is reprehensible.

As Juvenal does in the Latin poem, Dryden delineates the various heinous crimes women perpetrate on men—illegitimate heirs, abortions, infanticide, dependence on drugs, and murder of their husbands. A violent and cruel sex who make men powerless to control them, the women the men are attracted to as potential brides are fearless in their attempts to imitate men. Their manliness is an external indication of their misdirected desires:

> They turn Virago's, too; the Wrastler's toyl
> They try, and Smear their Naked Limbs with Oyl:
> Against the Post, their wicker Shields they crush,
> Flourish the Sword, and at the Plastron push.
> Of every Exercise the Mannish Crew
> Fulfils the Parts, and oft Excels us too:
> Prepar'd not only in feign'd Fights to'engage,
> But rout the Gladiators on the Stage. [ll. 346-53]

Juxtaposed to the literal images of effeminacy, the masculine Amazons desire the half-men:

> Behold the strutting *Amazonian* Whore,
> She stands in Guard with her right Foot before;
> Her Coats Tuck'd up; and all her Motions just,
> She stamps, and then Cries hah at every thrust:
> But laugh to see her tyr'd with many a bout,
> Call for the Pot, and like a Man Piss out. [ll. 365-70]

Dryden, following Juvenal, examines numerous examples of woman's power to kill. The satirist cautions the child to beware his own mother's food, for she cares more for his property than for his life. Yet the persona, edging toward tragedy, rather abruptly acknowledges that such topics make the poet forget "his Bus'ness is to Laugh and Bite" (l. 830). The apology is as soon forgotten, however, as he sharpens the barb against murdering mothers with the example of Drymon's wife. A modern Roman woman, unlike her ancient predecessors, she premeditates her crime. The pious women of antiquity may have exchanged their lives for those of their condemned husbands, but our women, writes the satirist, "Wou'd save their Lapdog sooner than their Lord" (l. 853). (Dryden's phrase anticipates Pope's in "Rape of the Lock.") Every modern woman is worse than a Clytemnaestra or a Belides, one of fifty sisters who killed their husbands on their wedding night:

> But Murther, now, is to perfection grown:
> And subtle Poysons are employ'd alone:
> Unless some Antidote prevents their Arts,
> And lines with Balsom all the Noble parts:
> In such a case, reserv'd for such a need,
> Rather than fail, the Dagger does the Deed. [ll. 858-63]

The outrageous conclusion to the satire insists that most women long to annihilate their husbands, and that marriage for Posthumous, who posed the initial question in the satire, would be a suicidal act. Juvenal's poem and Dryden's translation are diatribes against marriage, but only because lustful women relentlessly violate the sacrosanct domestic household and threaten the conjugal, economic, political, and religious order.

Dryden uses Juvenal's Sixth Satire to levy a vicious attack on women, without posing any alternatives and without suggesting that ideal women (with the notable exception of the *rara avis*) exist. He can present himself as the witty spokesman for ritualized aggression from the safe and apparently humane position of the translator who removes himself from the violence and obscenity of the original. The satire laments women's state without attempting moral reformation. The translation, with its frame of disavowal, is a paradigm for the ambivalence Restoration satirists displayed toward women—a document testifying not only to the sex's inherent inferiority but to their active malevolence against men. Though the satire was often translated in the eighteenth century and constantly cited as the prototype of misogyny, no other translation combined Dryden's explicit sexuality with contemporary references and generalizations about the whole sex from the portraits of particular women.

In an earlier translation, Sir Robert Stapylton had set the pattern for later translators, including Dryden, in disclaiming similarities between the women depicted in the satire and contemporary Englishwomen, "this Island being planted with such examples of valour in men, and chastity in women, as demonstrates that wee are as absolutely freed of the vanities and vices of the *Romans,* as of their yoke and servitude."[8] Robert Stapylton translated and published Juvenal's first six satires in 1644, and later published the complete satires in *Juvenal's Sixteen Satyrs, or Survey of the Manners and Actions of Mankind.*[9] The theme of Stapylton's translation closely follows Juvenal's text: the undesirability of marriage, the corruption of women, women's aping men, and the loss of sensuality. Including Juvenal's lusty details, Stapylton retains, for example, Juvenal's lines which recommend a young boy to Posthumous, who is about to marry to assuage his lust, and the description of Messalina, wife of the Emperor Claudius, is explicit. Throughout his text, Stapylton seems to assume that his task is to provide a faithful translation of Juvenal rather than to write a contemporary analysis of Englishwomen.

Another seventeenth-century version, translated by Barten Holyday, parallels Dryden's in length, with just over eight hundred lines.[10] The argument shifts the emphasis slightly from lust to the disparity between appearance and reality in the Roman ladies. The effect of keeping Roman names maintains the distance between the two periods. The references to specific Roman names follow Juvenal's lines more exactly than do Dryden's more general references to "one" or "another." The section on Messalina, reeking with lust, remains powerfully satiric and sensual. On the whole, Dryden's later version displays more skill in creating compact intensity. For example, here is Holyday's passage on drunken women returning from a night of revelry:

> Here's nothing feign'd; All's True: Enough to fire
> Old *Priamus,* and *Nestor's* maim'd desire.
> But when these very Women have all done,
> Impatiently from these Deceits they run.
> A Lover they'll not want; though Some do blind
> Nature's broad Light and Sin below their Kind! [p. 98]

Here is Dryden's clear and succinct attack:

> Impatient of delay, a general sound,
> An universal Groan of Lust goes round;
> For then, and only then, the Sex sincere is found.
> Now is the time of Action; now begin,
> They cry, and let the lusty Lovers in. [ll. 444-47]

In addition, Holyday tends to avoid the sweeping generalizations about the sex that Dryden uses as summaries for sections. Among these terse epithets are lines 395-96: "There's nothing bolder than a Woman Caught; / Guilt gives 'em Courage to maintain their Fault"; or lines 467-68: "The Sex is turn'd all Whore; they Love the Game; / And Mistresses, and Maids, are both the same." The effect that Dryden achieves is to turn the satire as much against the inherent characteristics of the sex as a whole as against luxury and marriage. Holyday, in contrast, simply leaves the derogatory portraits to speak for themselves and makes the flaws seem to be associated with the hideous individual acts which depict the exception to the rule of good women, as he suggests in his argument. Thus he retains the sexuality, includes the scatology, and avoids the generalizations which turn the satire against the whole sex of females.

Among the various eighteenth-century translations of

Juvenal are Henry Fielding's burlesque fragment (c. 1725 but later revised), Edward Burnaby Greene's expurgated version in 1763, and *The Adulteress,* a free paraphrase (1773).[11] Fielding's partial translation, probably his earliest writing, was supposedly a vengeful response to an unfortunate youthful love affair, though he clearly updated the topical references later in his life. He follows the conventions we have come to expect, denies any personal antifeminist sentiment, and indeed the preface to his 1743 *Miscellanies* (in which the fragment was included) begins with the disavowal: "My Modernization of Part of the Sixth Satire of *Juvenal,* will, I hope, give no Offence to that Half of our Species, for whom I have the greatest Respect and Tenderness." He continues, "For my Part, I am much more inclined to Panegyric on that amiable Sex, which I have always thought treated with very unjust Severity by ours, who censure them for Faults (if they are truly such) into which we allure and betray them, and of which we ourselves, with an unblamed Licence, enjoy the most delicious Fruits" (p. 3). No one who translates the misogynist satire wants to be called a misogynist, yet Fielding, like Dryden, makes Roman women's Greek affectations into Englishwomen's French ones; and Kitty Clive, Peg Woffington, Mother Haywood, and Pamela are all subjected to good-natured abuse. Fielding turns Ursidius into a cuckolded Theophilus Cibber and takes into his net other men as well as women, including Lord Lyttleton, William Pitt, and Lord Hervey, making the satire seem more like a satire on mankind. Throughout the much-abbreviated version in colloquial tetrameter couplets, Fielding steers away from hints of obscenity. He concludes abruptly because "the Remainder is in many Places too obscene for chaste Ears" (p. 117 n.3), so obscene that Juvenal's Latin could not be made applicable to Englishwomen.

To an even greater extent than Fielding's translation, Edward Greene's satire widely diverges from the Latin to soften the antifeminism. The criticisms of women relate to their folly in preferring Barry to Garrick and in indulging the popular taste for Italian music. Another eighteenth-century translation by Edward Owen, subtitled "A Looking-Glass for

the Ladies," much abbreviated to just over 560 lines, elimi-
nates the specific sexual details of Dryden's longer version
and employs a more casual diction.[12] For example, Dryden's
sentimental modern nymphs, Cynthia and Lesbia, "Who for a
Sparrow's Death dissolve in Tears," become even more pitiful: "Wives, not like Cynthia, or the nymph, who cry'd / Her
pretty eyes out when her sparrow died" (ll. 9–10). Owen
omits references to whoring; other details omitted include
urging Ursidius to assuage his lust with a boy rather than a
wife. In addition, women's incestuous desire for their fathers
is obscured; lines such as "many a fair Nymph has in a Cave
been spread, / And much good Love, without a Feather-Bed"
(ll. 85–86) are glossed over. "Looking-Glass" also omits details of the theater, references to abortion, dildoes, and
various sexual perversions.

In Owen's translation, the portrait of Hippia, whose lust
for a fencer exceeded her love for her husband and children,
closely parallels its antecedents. On the other hand, "A
Looking-Glass" greatly abbreviates the famed Messalina portrait as it strips Dryden's picture of the lusty harlot of its
sordid quality: "The steam of Lamps still hanging on her
Cheeks / In Ropy Smut" (ll. 187-88). Other less sexual portraits—Cessinia, desired for her wealth, and Bibula, for her
face—pose no threat to censorious minds and can be wholly
included. A description of a whoring mother who awaits her
"Panting Stallion at the Closet-Door" in Dryden becomes
"th'invited lover" in Owen's poem. "A Looking-Glass"
lamely calls Dryden's "strutting *Amazonian* Whore" a woman
who "aims the scientific thrust," and misses the ribaldry evi-
dent in Dryden's lines: "She stamps, and then Cries hah at
every thrust: / But laugh to see her tyr'd with many a bout, /
Call for the Pot, and like a Man Piss out" (ll. 368-70). Both
translators follow Juvenal in arguing that luxury caused the
disruption of domestic tranquillity. As in Dryden, the black
swan, the chaste and accomplished woman, offers potential
as the ideal wife in "A Looking-Glass," yet her very perfection presents as serious a threat as murdering women. Such a
wife takes pleasure in arbitrary and even cruel sway over the
lives of her inferiors; she can overpower husband after

husband. Dryden says, "To Absolute Dominion she aspires," while "Looking-Glass" makes the woman speak: "It is my sovereign will: who dares withstand?" The portrait explodes the myth of the ideal woman in both translations.

Dryden's poem is superior to "A Looking-Glass" in the quality of images, the fine details, and the power of the satire. The teeming portraits of Tullia and Laufella prove to be too obscene for Owen's translation. There are no lines corresponding to Dryden's lines 416-46 in the later poem. The effect is to make "A Looking-Glass" less an invective against women's lust and more a tirade against the power of wives to control men, to ruin their lives, and even to murder them. Thus the gist as well as some of the explicit portraits remain. Like Dryden's poem it ends with warnings about monstrous women who breed tragedy and kill those who would inherit what they want to claim, including their children, stepchildren, and husbands. There is no redemptive apology or excuse for the women. Dryden parallels Juvenal's apology for the tragic quality of the satire and proceeds to cite examples from "history"—Medea, Clytemnaestra, and others who prove his point. Edward Owen subjugates lust in women to cataloguing the vanities of unhappiness and worse that wives can wreak on their husbands. Woman offends most by disrupting the laws of inheritance and the husband's traditional control over her.

One of the best-known translations is that by William Gifford. Capable of vicious attack, as in his *Epistle to Peter Pindar* (1800), Gifford precedes his 998-line version with an argument in which he confidently asserts that Juvenal had a clear organizational pattern in mind, but he does not flinch from recognizing the antifeminism inherent in "a dreadful catalogue of enormities" in Juvenal's original.[13] He comments on Dryden's reputation for antifeminism: "Even Dryden, who was never suspected of sparing the sex, either in his poems or plays, deems it necessary to apologize here, and assures the world that he was compelled to translate this formidable Satire because 'no one else would do it'" (p. 159). Gifford then dissociates himself from attacking the modern Englishwoman: "The ashes of the ladies whose

actions are here recorded, have long been covered by the
Latin and Flaminian ways; nor have their follies, or their
vices, much similarity with those of modern times." If any
woman recognizes herself, he adds, let her reform, but most
women will share men's "indignant curiosity, on the representation of a profligate and abandoned race, not more
distant in time, than in every virtue and accomplishment,
from themselves" (p. 160).

Gifford takes his task as translator seriously, and he includes lengthy notes which chide Holyday, Stapylton, or
Owen for misunderstandings of Roman culture or Juvenal's
meaning. He praises Dryden's version as "a most noble effort
of genius." Like the translators other than Dryden, he
particularizes the satire with specific Roman names from
Juvenal, but Gifford's notes delineate, for example, the
history of Roman mime or customs of bathing or religious
ritual rather than focusing on the way satire attacks women.
He even defends the ladies at one point. In the lines which
describe women's salacious activities between the Megalisian
and Plebian shows, Gifford comments in a note, "The former
games were celebrated on the 5th of April, and the latter on
the 15th of November; so that here really was a long interval
to exercise the patience of the ladies" (p. 170 n.105). The
pissing dancing master is missing, as are Dryden's contemporary references to park, mall, playhouse, and court. Nor does
he include the blanket antifeminism of Dryden, that "Each
Inconvenience makes their Virtue cold: / But Womankind, in
Ills, is ever bold" (ll. 135-36). In Dryden, Hippia's lust overcoming her fear is generalized to a characteristic of the sex.
Gifford includes sexually explicit details, such as references
to homosexuality, incest, or the goldleaf on Messalina's
papillae, yet generalizations about the sex are much less
frequent than in Dryden. One exception occurs in the lines
following Messalina's portrait: "Women in judgment weak, in
feeling strong, / By every gust of passion borne along" (ll.
199-200). But lest there be any mistake about Gifford's
intentions, he provides a lengthy explanatory note discussing
the women of Juvenal's time. The footnotes reinforce the
idea that Juvenal was angered at particular historical ex-

amples and chose the satiric form to vent his spleen. Similarly, in a generalization about affected wives, Gifford parallels Dryden concerning women's control over their husbands: "Women no mercy to a lover show / Who once declares his passion; though they glow / With equal fires, no warm return they deign, / But triumph in his spoils,—but mock his pain" (ll. 317-20).

Gifford worries considerably about those wives who divorce multiple husbands, however, and concludes that Juvenal must not be taken literally: "The exclamation of Juvenal is merely a bitter sarcasm on the wives of his time, who were so lost to every sense of the ancient honour, as to be ready to perpetuate their want of chastity on their tombstones!" (p. 189 n.351). If there is any doubt that Gifford could be implicating Englishwomen, he again clarifies in a footnote that *Roman* women, not English, attempted to be fencers, fighters, and gladiators, and that they are so removed from early nineteenth-century England as to require historical verification. Whatever epithets attacking the sex as a whole Gifford includes, he disavows with clarifying footnotes.

Gifford, then, is no less obscene than Dryden or Juvenal, though he is always quick to differentiate the present from Juvenal's Roman past. Reviewers took him much to task for his vulgar and indecent language, as well as the inelegance of many a poetic line.[14] But the criticism levied against him did not accuse him of attempting to degrade, or even to refer to, the contemporary Englishwoman. Gifford apparently succeeded in conveying the impression that he was translating an artifact, and his weak Alexandrine angered the critics as much as his offensive language. The *Critical Review* wrote, "Our modest translator veils *one* indelicate word by this lone, lame, unauthorized, and filthy Alexandrine"; and in his 1806 translation, Gifford revised the offending lines from "At break of day / Thou to the levee go'st, and, on the way, / Wadst through the plashy scene of thy chaste moiety's play" to "You pass, aroused at dawn, you court to pay, / The loathsome scene of their licentious play."[15] Thus Gifford's translation relishes Juvenal's coarse and vulgar wit, and even in his revised edition makes no attempt to turn an attack on Roman luxury, lust, marriage, and women into a veiled moral treatise addressed to the contemporary feminists such as Anna Laetitia Barbauld, Mary Hays, Mary "Perdita" Robinson, and Mary Wollstonecraft.

Finally, Francis Hodgson in his translation of 1807 acknowledges Holyday, Dryden, Owen, and Gifford in his preface, yet he criticizes their attempts to cram Latin hexameters into English heroic poetry. In fact, he notes, "The consequence of Holyday's passion for literal translation was, that he neither wrote sense nor poetry."[16] Hodgson adopts a protective attitude toward the ladies, and claims that Juvenal is "a most improper study for them." Yet he does not say anything about obscenity or about the Sixth Satire in particular. In the argument Hodgson blames "Juvenal's attitude" on his bachelorhood and urges the reader to pity rather than condemn Juvenal's savagery. He takes issue with Gifford's belief that the satire's organization is methodical, and unlike Gifford, Hodgson insists that lust is the central theme: "Juvenal therefore, in my opinion, followed no other method in this satire than that of making lust the most prominent object upon his canvas—and all the subordinate passions, as they . . . recurred to his memory, he ranged around their chief; but in the rapidity of composition, left them to find their own places."

Hodgson's translation resembles "A Looking-Glass for the Ladies" in its mild tenor and even in its colloquial diction. The portrait of Messalina, for example, lacks the specific lewdness of Dryden's translation:

> She last retreated from the reeking den,
> Though quite worn out, unsatisfied with men;
> And black all over with the brothel's fume,
> And flaming with the madness of her womb,
> Climb'd, unabash'd, again th'imperial bed,
> And by the world's great master laid her head.

Like "Looking-Glass," Hodgson's version avoids explicit sexuality but is not squeamish about urine or vomit. Women are unquestionably the object of strong satire because they violate men's expectations of them as mothers, wives, and patriots. While Juvenal in Dryden's translation emphasizes the tragic nature of the satire and his fidelity to the real world of experience, Hodgson uses the same lines to disavow connection with England's ladies: "But this is all a dream—and I, who sing / Beyond the height of any ancient song, / To Satire's must the tragic buskin give, / And write not of the land in which I live." And like all translators, Hodgson allows the poem to conclude with the threat of new Belides and new Clytemnaestras ever ready to kill for lust. Again, then, the sexually explicit details are softened, the satire affects to exclude Englishwomen from its province, and Hodgson simply omits the most obscene passages from the poem.

Most of the translations of the Sixth Satire are funny, lively, and entertaining. They also keep alive an especially virulent tradition of misogyny, or antifeminist assumptions and conventions. The movement from private offenders against moral laws to public offenders, the attention to pleasure (whether sexual or the pleasure of leisure), the fear of women's power, the stereotypes of the vain coquette, the affected learned lady, the Amazonian imitator of men, the religious infidel—all are aspects of Juvenal's satire which came to exert a powerful influence on the literary tradition of antifeminism as it was revived in the various translations. Dryden's ambiguous attitude, framed as it is by an argument which craftily affects dissociation from contemporary women, and charged as it is by subtle allusions to the similarities between English and Roman women, provides a fertile field for Jonathan Swift, Alexander Pope, and minor eighteenth-century satirists to explore and extend. Juvenal's Sixth Satire was never far from the minds of eighteenth-century writers, and we should not be surprised to discover that Mr. Supple, curate of Mr. Allworthy's parish, in Henry Fielding's *Tom Jones* (1749), mentions the lines from the Sixth Satire when he announces that the pregnant Molly Seagrim, Tom Jones's sordid wench, appeared in church in one of Sophia's dresses.[17]

By the middle of the eighteenth century, the obscenity of Juvenal's original is tempered, the protests are loud that no Englishwomen are attacked, and positive examples that are the exemplars to their sex begin to intrude on the image of a whole sex of whores. The interplay between the two—the wicked and the good—sets up a crux of possibilities for the sex. The ideal woman, so obviously omitted from Juvenal and Dryden, intrudes on the fiction of antifeminist satire and forecasts a change in the myth at mid-eighteenth century—for to pose an ideal woman suggests the possibility that not *all* women are evil, and it implies that lust, lechery, and inconstancy may not be characteristics of the sex, but are rather characteristics of that portion of the sex which has not been reformed. As the blame shifts from woman's inherent sexual characteristics to her social plight, the path from the whore to the fallen woman is a path toward greater understanding and greater sympathy for the sex.

VI

"The Sex's Flight":
Women and Time
in Swift's Poetry

Jonathan Swift, one of the most notorious eighteenth-century satirists against women, largely separates the good woman from the wicked in his satires. Swift's most extensive treatment of women appears in the early odes, the birthday poems to Stella, and the cluster of scatological poems written from 1727 to 1733, ranging from the panegyrical praise of Mrs. Biddy Floyd to the harsh condemnation of "A Beautiful Young Nymph Going to Bed." With the notable exception of the poems on Stella, Swift's early poems repeat the Juvenalian convention that the ideal woman has vanished into an ancient past which he calls into the present with Christian and classical allusions. "Strephon and Chloe," for example, opens with references to the myth of woman as a phoenix who arises on a miraculous occasion: "Of Chloe *all* the Town has rung; / By ev'ry size of Poets sung: / So beautiful a Nymph appears / But once in Twenty Thousand Years" (ll. 1-4).[1] Only in his earlier poems does Swift allow an ideal woman to intrude into the satires on the sex, as in "Cadenus and Vanessa" and "To Lord Harley," an early ode. The ideal woman of the earlier poems is panegyrical; the ideal woman of the Stella poems has human imperfections and claims existence in the real world.

In an ode on the marriage of the Lord Treasurer's son to
Lady Henrietta Cavendish Holles, "To Lord Harley since Earl
of Oxford on His Marriage" (1713), a virtuous woman stands
as an emblem of a social order that reminds men of the more
glorious past of the sex. Swift twists the Daphne-Apollo
myth to an extreme. In the original myth and in Dryden's
translation (for which Swift had no fondness), Cupid's anger
incites Apollo's passionate, self-consuming fire of love.
Images that describe Apollo, the god of wit, learning, and
light, emphasize his bestiality in pursuit of his female prey,
the unwilling virgin Daphne. Apollo seems to be a proud,
lustful lover who longs to violate the wild freedom of the
chaste nymph; he even smacks his lips in lustful anticipation
and hopes a sharp thorn will pierce her foot to slacken her
pace. The unfortunate Daphne prays for metamorphosis and
is transformed into a laurel tree. Having sacrificed everything
except her smooth skin to the cause of chastity, she passively
accepts Apollo's consolatory gift of perpetually green
branches, "Unfading as th'Immortal Pow'rs above." She even
shakes the branches in happy affirmation of the newly established discordant harmony. But in Swift's treatment, in spite
of Apollo's love for Daphne, she flees from him:

> Had Bacchus after Daphne reel'd,
> The Nymph had soon been brought to yield;
> Or, had Embroider'd Mars pursu'd,
> The Nymph would ne'er have been a prude.
> Ten thousand footsteps, full in view,
> Mark out the way where Daphne flew.
> For such is all the sex's flight,
> They fly from learning, wit, and light:
> They fly, and none can overtake
> But some gay coxcomb, or a rake. [ll. 13-22]

The whole sex seeks escape from a terrifying union with a
Lord Harley, the masculine Apollonian ideal, but the poem
goes on to distinguish Harley's young bride from the
frightened Daphne, and thus the poem becomes a compli-

ment to Lady Cavendish. Swift twists the myth: not Lady Cavendish but "that glitt'ring crowd" of fleeing virgins is turned into blocks of wood. Athena "stupify'd them all to stocks." All lose their substance, and because they frenetically avoid choosing Apollonian virtues, they are transformed to less than what they might be. The poet praises Lady Cavendish at the expense of her sex:

> Terrestrial nymphs, by formal arts,
> Display their various nets for hearts:
> Their looks are all by method set,
> When to be prude and when coquette;
> Yet, wanting skill and pow'r to chuse,
> Their only pride is to refuse. [ll. 53-58]

Marriage requires a choice and even a metamorphosis.

What Swift satirizes in his poems on women is what offends him in other aspects of eighteenth-century society. As Denis Donoghue has aptly remarked, "As a poet he distrusts the vague, transitional moments when a thing is neither fully itself nor something else. He is restless with things that do not maintain their own identity." All that Swift finds intolerable—"the unconscious, sleep, dreams, visions of fancy, delusions of pride, the passions"[2]—is particularly associated with women in the satiric tradition.

The sensitive moral implications of a woman's misusing her entire lifetime are explicit in William Law's *A Serious Call to a Devout and Holy Life* (1729), a book much recommended for the education of young ladies in the eighteenth century. Law presents a pairing of two sisters, Flavia and Miranda, and he details the way in which each apportions her time. Time, Law cautions, is "too precious to be disposed of by chance, and left to be devoured by any thing that happens in his way. If he [a man] lays himself under a necessity of observing how every day goes through his hands, and obliges himself to a certain order of time in his *business,* his *retirements,* and *devotions,* it is hardly to be imagined, how soon such a conduct would reform, improve, and perfect the whole course of his life."[3] Flavia takes little care of her time: half her life is wasted in bed and the other half "will have been consumed in eating, drinking, dressing, visiting, conversation, reading, and hearing Plays and Romances, at Opera's, Assemblies, Balls, and Diversions."[4] She squanders her days in useless self-absorbed activity, never accounting for her time or turning toward others. Miranda, on the other extreme, lives in pious harmony and exquisite symmetry. God rewards good women with sainthood in eternity if they conduct their lives on earth with respect for time. But most women in Swift's poetry are Flavia-like in allowing themselves to be buffeted by time rather than seeking to redeem it.

Antifeminist Thomas Brown similarly pairs the characters of virtuous women with their less modest counterparts in *A Legacy for the Ladies* (1705), and women's misuse of time is a constant theme. He writes of women who waste their lives gaming,

> and from an Hour employ'd at it, one comes to spend a whole Life; and this is done without thinking on it, much less after 'tis once done; for time runs away so easily at it, that for want of observing it, the Loss is without *Redemption*; the Term of our Lives finishes, and ... of so many Moments that we had at our Disposal, there remains but one to regret all others in. In this last we have so much Sight as serves to punish us, it's small space contains the *Idea* of all the others, and the Sight of that infinite Number of the pass'd wasted Moments, makes us sensible of the *Eternity* of the *Time* to come, when we shall answer for every ill spent Moment of our Lives.[5]

Swift's "An Answer to a Scandalous Poem, Wherein the Author most audaciously presumes to cast an indignity upon their Highnesses the *CLOUDS,* by comparing them to a *WOMAN*" (1732), delivered in the person of a cloud named Chief Dermot O'Nephely, is a response to Thomas Sheridan's "A New Simile for the Ladies, with Useful Annotations." Clouds are renowned for their constancy, he argues, and to compare them to women is an unforgivable insult to the clouds: "You'll see a *Cloud* in gentle Weather / Keep the same Face an Hour together: / While Women, if it could be reckon'd, / Change ev'ry Feature, ev'ry Second" (ll. 39-42). The light poems mock feminine transience with easy good humor, but the profound distaste Swift felt for lack of control underlies the pleasantry. Even more specifically, women, speeding toward their doom, fail to control their daily lives. A day in the life of most women, according to Swift and his contemporaries, is a day misspent.

Apparently Stella's death in 1728 precipitated a series of deeply moral and occasionally obscene poems on women. Lady Acheson, Swift's sometime friend at Market Hill, is often the subject of satire rather than panegyric. In "An Epistle to a Lady" (1733) Lady Acheson wistfully complains of her childhood training which causes her to float above temporal limitations in her whirl of activity:

> Bred a Fondling, and an Heiress;
> Drest like any Lady May'ress;
> Cockered by the Servants round,
> Was too good to touch the Ground:
> Thought the Life of ev'ry Lady
> Shou'd be one continu'd Play-Day:
> Balls, and Masquerades, and Shows,
> Visits, Plays, and Powder'd Beaux. [ll. 35-42]

The lines imply the lady's lack of awareness of anything but the present moment, and they ridicule her inability to account for the passing of the days. She stands at the opposite end of the spectrum from an ideal woman like William Law's Miranda, who rises early for devotion, welcomes the day as an opportunity for renewed pious dedication to God, and never knows boredom.

Swift hints at society's responsibility in contributing to the emptiness of women's lives, but the onus falls on the individual woman to escape from the chaos of unredeemed time. In many of Swift's scatological poems, including "A Beautiful Young Nymph Going to Bed" (1731) and "The Lady's Dressing Room" (1730), a woman's day displays a microcosm of the waste of her life. The waste may be occasioned by perverse inability to make order from mad chaos, or it may arise from sloth. Every woman's first daily activity is a time-consuming attempt to make order, however tenuous, from her chaotic state. The filth which Strephon discovers in "The Lady's Dressing Room" is the unseemly residue from Celia's five long hours preparatory to presenting herself to the public. The only certainty in the chaos of the room is the pervasive odor of Celia's excrement, and Strephon "smelt it all the Time before" (l. 82).

The two Swift satires which depict woman's daily inappropriate use of leisure with greatest particularity are "The Furniture of a Woman's Mind" (1727) and "The Journal of a Modern Lady" (1729). In both poems the satirist characterizes women as wasting time with incessant chattering and repeating the same meaningless activities each day. The tiresome lady of "Furniture of a Woman's Mind" sits long hours with a coxcomb and mindlessly rattles stale witticisms. Every woman "Can, at her Morning Tea, run o'er / The Scandal of the Day before. / Improving hourly in her Skill, / To cheat and wrangle at Quadrille" (ll. 23-26). She manipulates her environment and turns time to her own treacherous advantage, and "By frequent Practice learns the Trick / At proper Seasons to be sick" (ll. 39-40). Her memory of the past teems with scandal, her present is an exercise in trickery, her future will bring declining beauty paralleled by greater adeptness at camouflaging her aging face.

Like Pope's "Epistle to a Lady," addressed to Martha Blount, "The Journal of a Modern Lady" ostensibly was written at a woman's request when Lady Acheson asked Swift for a satire on women. The day filled with trivia belatedly begins when milady awakens at noon. Lingering over her tea until four o'clock, she postpones dinner to finish dressing. From four until six o'clock, the ladies talk incessantly, as ninety-six lines imitate the chatter. The din frightens away discretion and modesty, and the reader almost flees as well: "They contradict, affirm, dispute, / No single Tongue one Moment mute" (ll. 177-78). The poem ends where it begins: the modern lady retires "With empty

Purse and aching Head." Her past is a memory of cards, her present an anticipation of future games. The activity of her day protects her from confronting experience, and it isolates her from meaningful exchange with the larger social order. Spinning in ever narrower circles, unconscious of the present moment, she propels herself toward doom.

Swift's portrayal of the state of modern woman shows that her failure to choose to redeem the moment finally causes her to fail to give her lifetime meaning. Her ignoring the passage of time becomes a futile attempt to deny beauty's transience and her body's decay. The external façade of woman's beauty soon crumbles, and the foolish beau who assumes that physical beauty is permanent will be tricked or get a pox; at worst he endangers his soul. Swift repeats the theme in "A Letter to a Young Lady on Her Marriage" (1723) when he cautions that "You will, in Time, grow a Thing indifferent, and perhaps contemptible, unless you can supply the Loss of Youth and Beauty with more durable Qualities. You have but a very few Years to be young and handsome in the Eyes of the World; and as few Months to be so in the Eyes of a Husband, who is not a Fool."[6] The same idea is rendered in the concluding lines of "Strephon and Chloe" (1731): "Rash Mortals, e'er you take a Wife, / Contrive your Pile to last for Life; / Since Beauty scarce endures a Day, / And Youth so swiftly glides away" (ll. 301-04).

Two of Swift's poems capture and hold in stasis a temporally defined period in the life of a woman, "The Progress of Beauty" (1719) and "The Progress of Marriage" (1721-22). The "progress form," familiar to Swift, was particularly appropriate to the subject because it suggests moving onward, sometimes toward an improved state of being, though in these poems the women progress toward whoredom and disaster. The first poem passes through a day which symbolizes a woman's lifetime, and the second traces the history of a marriage. In the inverted form of "The Progress of Beauty," Celia awakens in filthy disrepair. After a short-lived period of deception, she rots into her final diseased decay. The moon's rising is compared to Celia's awakening, though Diana, like Celia, appears only when the day begins to wane. Having risen in ugly disarray, Celia uses "Pencil, Paint, and Brush" to restore artificial order: "Thus after four important Hours / Celia's the Wonder of her Sex" (ll. 53-54). She cements her face, makes time stable, and, modeling herself on Diana, shines from a distance. Her time of beauty, however, is only a day or the brief span of a month. Without substantial form, woman soon fades; the natural decay of the waning moon parallels the mechanical rotting of Celia. At the month's half-way point Diana evidences signs of dissolving and disappearing: Yet as she wasts, she grows discreet, / Till Midnight never shows her Head; / So rotting Celia stroles the Street / When sober Folks are all a-bed" (ll. 101-04).

Mercury, who combines the duties of messenger of the gods and escort of the dead, and for whom the quicksilver substance thought to cure venereal disease is named, is foe to both the lunar and the mortal ladies. It is in vain to fight him, for woman's life of beauty endures only briefly, and fleeting time is woman's enemy: "Ye Pow'rs who over Love preside, / Since mortal Beautyes drop so soon, / If you would have us well supply'd, / Send us new Nymphs with each new Moon" (ll. 117-20). If beauty fades, a woman must find other, more frightening means of maintaining tyranny over the masculine sex. Pope warns of "a whole Sex of Queens! / Pow'r all their end, but Beauty all the means" (ll. 219-20).

If women are exposed for what they are, their power diminishes, and deception becomes more difficult after marriage. One way to protract the illusion which perpetuates woman's power is for a young woman to marry an older man. In a second progress poem, "The Progress of Marriage" (1721-22), the ill-conceived, disharmonious union between an aged dean and a young coquette ends in revelation of what inevitably results from the deception—his death and her impending decay. In the first of two parts of "Progress of Marriage," the poem traces a day in the mismatched time schemes of the bride and groom, while the second section records the abrupt termination of the brief marriage. The "dull divine," past fifty, values money and longs for an heir; the young bride loves bustling activity. Their happiness extends through the wedding day. She, like Swift's other giddy ladies, takes tea at noon, shops and chatters the afternoon away, dines at four, bustles off to a play and a masquerade at nine, and returns exhausted to her sleeping husband at five in the morning. He, on the other hand, plods through the parson's measured routine of rising early and arriving home when his wife departs: "He like an orderly Divine / Comes home a quarter after nine, / And meets her hasting to the Ball, / Her Chairmen push him from the Wall" (ll. 83-86). Having been married a year without an heir, they fly to Bath in search of fertility, but "The Dean with all his best Endeavour / Gets not an Heir, but gets a Feaver" (ll. 151-52), which causes his death. The "progress" of the marriage ends with the poet's wish for Lady Jane's exposure to the pox from her new lovers. "A rooted Pox to last for ever" would provide the single constant in her self-serving life.

In several ways Swift's despicable women forecast the end of man's time. A *memento mori* not only predicts man's death—she may contribute to it. Strephon, frightened of his mistress's perfect beauty, reflects that he might die from the lightning shot from Chloe's eyes (l. 110). Women may exhaust men with their giddy activities, sexual and nonsexual, like the young coquette in "The Progress of Marriage." A more frequently recurring theme is the deluding woman who may infect man with venereal disease. Swift treats the serious subject good-naturedly in the poem which distinguishes women from clouds. Dermot O'Nephely poses the contrast in a rhetorical question:

> Some Critick may object, perhaps,
> That *Clouds* are blam'd for giving *Claps*;
> But, what alas are *Claps* Aetherial,
> Compar'd for Mischief, to Venereal?
> Can *Clouds* give Bubo's, Ulcers, Blotches,
> Or from your Noses dig out Notches? [ll. 15-20]

But the subject elsewhere receives more serious treatment. In "On the Women About Town" (1704), Rochester writes,

"They carry a fate which no man can oppose: / The loss of his heart and the fall of his nose" (ll. 9-10).[7] The heat and frenzy of passion may bring death, and woman may thus cut short man's time on earth. Cassinus fears that Celia's beauty may be distorted by the pox, the poet wishes a pox on Lady Jane in "The Progress of Marriage," and Celia ("The Progress of Beauty") wastes away from disease.

Most significantly, women may also cause spiritual death, and Swift's poems warn men not to be tempted to seek their eternity in women. In a sense women never progressed in time after mankind's fall; they remain trapped in stasis between a golden past and future immortality. All their energies must be directed toward providing a false and elusive façade of constancy in order to create hope of eternity, and men long to be deceived in the passionate moment which annihilates time. But most women, Swift seeks to remind disbelieving men, walk with death. Cassinus has fantasies of dying from Celia's power: "And on the Marble grave these Rhimes, / A Monument to after-Times: / 'Here *Cassy* lies, by *Caelia* slain, / And dying, never told his Pain'" (ll. 75-78). Woman's power to hasten death is most explicitly stated in "Death and Daphne" (1730), addressed to Lady Acheson. Death seeks a bride to perpetuate his kind, and coquettes adorn him in his disguise of a beau. So taken with Death's appearance that she forgets "what is Trumps," Daphne attempts to win him with her witty allusions to Death's domain: "She fancy'd, those *Elysian* Shades / The sweetest Place for Masquerades: / How pleasant on the Banks of Styx, / To troll it in a Coach and Six!" (ll. 85-88). When Death reaches for her hand, however, he finds it "dry and cold as Lead." Her touch even offends Death, and he flees. Woman, it seems, may be more frightening than death itself.

Usually, however, Swift associates the female sex with folly rather than death. "A Beautiful Young Nymph Going to Bed" (1734) strips a woman of our illusions about her and reduces her to her various ugly parts. The poem relies on commonplace assumptions about women, particularly "dressing-room poems," and if we place it in the context of satires against women, it increases our understanding of

Swift's adoption of a poetic attitude toward the sex and his concepts about the nature of the sex.

Juvenal's Sixth Satire apparently served as an important source for all subsequent dressing-room scenes like that represented in Swift's "A Beautiful Young Nymph." In his translation of the antifeminist satire, Dryden acknowledges that the original has become "a Common-place, from whence all the Moderns have notoriously stollen their sharpest Raileries."[8] A central scene that Dryden and other moderns appropriated from Juvenal is the intimate revelation of a woman's dressing room: in the Sixth Satire the Roman wife, attended by servants, frantically prepares to meet her lover at the shrine of Isis, goddess of fertility. Here is Dryden's version: "For if she hasts abroad to take the Ayr, / Or goes to *Isis* Church, (the Bawdy, House of Pray'r), / She hurries all her Handmaids to the Task; / Her Head, alone, will twenty Dressers ask" (ll. 627-30). The lady's dressing ritual is self-worship, just as Belinda's dressing in Pope's "Rape of the Lock" is a narcissistic rite. She arms herself for her adulterous lover. The lady imitates the erection of a military fortification when she creates her elaborate coiffeur. The dressing of her hair is as painstaking and deliberate as the protection of her honor: "Such Counsel, such delib'rate care they take, / As if her Life and Honour lay at stake, / With Curls, on Curls, they build her Head before; / And mount it with a Formidable Tow'r" (ll. 643-46). The satirist assures us, however, that the self-inflated woman can be disarmed. We need only see her from another perspective, the rear, to perceive how ridiculous she is: "but, look behind, / And then she dwindles to the Pigmy kind" (ll. 647-48).

There are other seventeenth- and early eighteenth-century references to Juvenal as providing the genesis for subsequent dressing-room scenes. In the "Fop-Dictionary, or An Alphabetical Catalogue of the . . . Terms of the Art Cosmetick . . ." (1690), the author, almost certainly Mary Evelyn, defines *Septizonium,* a word used in the dressing-room poem that precedes the dictionary, with reference to Juvenal: "*Septizonium.* A very high Tower in Rome, built by the Emperour *Severus,* of Seven Ranks of Pillars, set one upon the other, and diminishing to the Top, like the Ladies new Dress for thier [*sic*] Heads, which was the mode among the *Roman* Dames, and is exactly describ'd by *Juvenal* in his 6th Satyr."[9] The author of *The Art of Knowing Women: or, the Female Sex Dissected* (1730) quotes Dryden's translation of Juvenal and adds, "Nothing can be more judicious, than JUVENAL'S *Ideas,* when he introduces us to a *Lady* at her TOILET, attended by her Chamber-Maid, in the greatest Confusion for want of Time to dress her self."[10] Similar passages appear in almost every antifeminist poem and pamphlet in the last thirty years of the seventeenth century. Another example, *Whipping Tom: or, A Rod for a Proud Lady,* chastises women for tempting men's basest instincts since "our nice and mincing Dames in *England,* spend their whole Lives for the most part in the Study and Care of decking, painting, and beautifying themselves, with such gaudy Habits, as if they intended to make the Tempter of *Eve,* fall in Love with 'em."[11]

The dressing-room scene from Juvenal evokes all that men found most frightening about the changing Restoration woman. It unites the three most frequent charges against the sex—pride, lust, and inconstancy. The dressing-room scenes warn men to penetrate the disguises of women in order to protect themselves. Since the boudoir is the site of woman's preparation for attacking and destroying men, to penetrate it is to disarm the woman. The dressing room, however, is also morbidly fascinating, and the boudoir becomes a living metaphor for a woman's mystery. A woman standing before her dressing table is engaged in exploring her sexual and psychic independence as she creates a separate, private, and self-glorified identity. A man's surreptitious entrance into the forbidden territory subverts her independence in the name of destroying vice.

The dressing-room poem culminates in Swift's satiric poems on women, particularly "A Lady's Dressing Room" (1730) and "A Beautiful Young Nymph Going to Bed" (1734). Swift is indebted to the unrelenting tone of Juvenal's Sixth Satire and its seventeenth-century interpretations. Like Juvenal he proposes to destroy the erotic potential of a whore, though he emphasizes her lust and pride rather than her inconstancy. Swift is within the Juvenalian tradition, as well as the native English antifeminist tradition, not only in inspiration, but in explicit grisly detail.

But Swift's poems are not so much warnings against marriage as against the folly of love, and it is here that they seem to imply more moral intentions than Juvenal or the seventeenth-century tradition. Revelation of the dressing room protects man from marriage; it also protects him from his own folly and vain imaginings. Again there is considerable precedent. Edward Ward, for example, stressed the power man can usurp by discovering woman's base nature in *Female Policy Detected* (1695): "Many in rich Ornaments look inviting, whose Beauty, when they undress, flies away with their Apparel, and leaves you ... a cloudy Mistress to embrace. If you like a Woman, and would discover if she be in Nature, what she may seem by Art, surprize her in a Morning undrest, and it is Ten to One but you will find your Goddess hath shifted off her Divinity, and the Angel you so much admir'd turn'd into a Magmallion"[12] (*magma* being the crusty dregs left after a liquid evaporates).

Swift himself announces a similar inspiration for "A Beautiful Young Nymph Going to Bed," though it has not been remarked by scholars. The source is Ovid's *Remedia Amoris: "Pars minima est ipsa Puella sui,"* as cited in the original title but omitted even in Harold Williams's edition.[13] Ovid comically offers a literal remedy for love, a poem of advice to supply both sexes with an antidote to the madness of romantic feelings. He recommends distracting oneself with money problems, seeking the diversions of the country, engaging fervently in business pursuits, and avoiding idleness. The poet's voice resounds with the confidence of his own experience. He takes care to direct his advice to those who seek relief from the pain of excessive passion, not to those who love freely and happily. There is good-natured urgency in his advice: the madness of love may lead to murder or suicide, and the poem intends to counteract that possibility. The psychological advice is aimed at restoring mental health. To impede its powerful disconcerting force, the poet recommends altering one's perceptions of the loved one. He cautions, "Faults too lie near to charms; by that error virtues oft were blamed for vices. Where you can, turn to the worse your girl's attractions, and by a narrow margin criticise amiss." He continues, "Her gait is awkward? take her for a walk; her bosom is all breasts? let no bands conceal the fault. If her teeth are ugly, tell her something to make her laugh; are her eyes weak? recount a tearful tale. It will profit, too, of a sudden, when she has not prepared herself for anyone, to speed of a morning to your mistress. We are won by dress; all is concealed by gems and gold; a woman is the least part of herself." The advice is to adopt the undressing role of the satirist: "Arrive unexpectedly: safe yourself, you will catch her unarmed; she will fall, hapless woman, by her own defects."[14] The stench of her cosmetics, her art, will hasten her fall from the lover's esteem.

Ovid's advice is not intended as a rake's conduct book, but rather as a comic manual for overcoming the disorienting effects of passion. Swift's "A Beautiful Young Nymph Going to Bed" shares common themes with Ovid's *Remedia Amoris.* To see the beautiful young nymph, Corinna, disarmed, is to avoid being deceived and to avoid love's disease. Imagining one's mistress alone in bed helps a lover avoid imagining a rival and thus reviving competitive emotions; and Swift's Corinna writhes in isolation. Ovid's pervasive tone, however, is that of a physician whose poem heals the lovesick; our last glimpse of "Corinna dizend" nauseates and poisons us.

The Ovidian allusion is curious and provides the comic context, though it is finally not as illuminating as the English tradition in understanding Swift's "A Beautiful Young Nymph." Bonamy Dobrée first suggested that Swift's poems on women may derive from an acknowledged tradition of antifeminist commonplaces, and other scholars have uncovered a number of seventeenth-century analogues. Among the anticipations of Swift's dressing-room scenes are Thomas Killigrew's *Parson's Wedding* (c. 1639), Evelyn's *Mundus Muliebris* (1690), Roger L'Estrange's translation of *Visions of Quevedo* (1702), and Joseph Thurston's *The Toilette* (1730), as well as a cluster of lesser burlesques.[15] But none is as closely parallel as the witty and obscene antifeminist replay of issues commonplace at the end of the century, Richard Ames's *Folly of Love* (1691).[16] This satire contradicts Katharine M. Rogers's contention that Swift's attacking romantic ideals of love, motherhood, and the physical functions "was extraordinary in the misogynistic satire of Swift's period, which generally consisted of ridicule of feminine foibles." She continues, "Even in the tradition, there are few precedents for his emphasis on the unpleasant details of female animality."[17]

A more recent critic, Ellen Pollak has briefly but convincingly argued that Swift's misogyny is less the result of his own neurosis or pathology than "a reflection of his failure to come to terms with the conventions 'modern' culture made available to him for writing about the female sex"[18]—in other words, Swift made the best of what was available to him and used the scatological tradition for original, but not primarily misogynist, purposes. As I indicate here, Swift's antifeminist posture and his obscene language are not at all original; what *is* original, and worth our careful scrutiny, is the use he makes of the various traditions in composing the poetry that startles us when it is removed from its context. Part of that context is Ames's satire (as well as those of Oldham, Robert Gould, and the other antifeminist curses discussed earlier), and here it deserves examination before I remark on its relevance to Swift.

Richard Ames writes the *Folly of Love* to deliver himself "from Love and Dotage." He attacks the sex as a whole, "the *Worlds great Plague,*" in order to prevent men from succumbing to women's lust, pride, and inconstancy. The satire begins with a remarkable turn on the traditional creation story. Eve's pregnancy precedes the Fall, and her eating of the forbidden fruit is attributed to a craving. Eve resembles the apple she eats: "Like *Sodom's Apples* pleasant to the Eye, / Within pale rottenness, and ashes lye" (p. 4). Though woman's exterior beguiles man, within that appearance she threatens physical and spiritual death. Beneath a woman's seeming beauty lies the ugliness that can destroy men.[19] Woman's artful pride shows itself in her excessive concern for cosmetics and clothes. Men, however, cannot be convinced of the flaws of their mistresses. As in Ovid, love may distort a young man's perceptions: "If she with Moles and *Spots* be larded o're, / He'l tell you *Venus* had a Mole before; / . . . If *Tawdry* and *Ill-drest,* she's *Modish* thought, / For Love can make a *Venus* of a *Slut*" (p. 25). Herein lies the danger of love, a danger of the imagination which helps perpetuate female follies. The only solution the poet sees is to create an entirely new society, and he concludes with the Utopian vision, a prelapsarian garden which includes choice wine, select friends, and womanless procreation. The state would then be peaceful and changeless, and man would have freed himself from his own partially self-imposed tyranny:

> We'd live, and could we Procreate like Trees, ⎫
> And without *Womans Aid*—   ⎬
> Promote and Propagate our *Species*;   ⎭
> The Day in Sports and innocent Delight
> We'd spend, and in soft *Slumber* wast the Night
> Sometimes within a private *Grotto* meet,
> With gen'rous Wines and Fruit our selves we'd Treat;
> Ambition, Envy, and that Meager Train,
> Could never interrupt our Peaceful *Raign*;
> Blest with *Strong-Health,* and a most quiet mind, ⎫
> Each day our *Thoughts* should new Diversion find, ⎬
> But *never, never* think on *Woman-kind.* [pp. 26-27] ⎭

The satirist's end, then, is to release men from the power of women by attacking the entire sex. Men need to free themselves from the power of the *sex*. Ideally men will learn to live without women, who only confuse them, prove them fools, and then destroy them.

Ames's description of a lady's returning from the playhouse, the center of disguise, strikingly parallels Swift's description of a prostitute disrobing. Both ladies are lovelorn—Ames's disappointed lady and Swift's Corinna, pride of Drury Lane, who strolls the streets without success. Here is Ames's account:

Imagin now from Play-house just return'd
A Lady, who when there, in fancy burn'd;
Uneasy by some disappointments made,
Preparing to undress her self for Bed;
Her curled Locks (mistaken for her own)
Are in confusion on her Toylet thrown;
Next her Glas Eye put nicely in a Box,
With Ivory Tooth, which never had the *Pox,*
Her stiff *Steel-Bodies,* which her *Bunch* did hide,
Are with her artificial *Buttocks* laid aside;
Thus she who did but a small hour ago,
Like *Angel* or *Terrestrial Goddess* show,
Slides into loathsom sheets, where since we've fixther,
Leave her, of *Pride* and *Lust,* an equal mixture. [p. 7]

Swift provides more explicit detail and of course the better poem. He chooses the midnight hour, an appropriate hour of metamorphosis, to expose the nymph's undressing. The order and content parallel Ames's *Folly of Love.* Both women first remove their hair, then their artificial eye. Swift elaborates on Ames's description of the ritual: Corinna's eye requires a wife to clean off oozing remnants of body fluids. Corinna lays aside her mouse-hide eyebrows and unfurls them before pressing them in her playbook. Instead of one pox-free ivory tooth, Corinna removes wires, cheek plumpers, and a whole set of false teeth. In both poems the woman's falsely padded breasts resume their natural sag as steel corset and false hip-paddings fall away, and the lady slides into slimy sheets. The poem moves from order to greasy chaos, from loneliness to desperate isolation. After a night of anguished imaginings, Corinna awakens to a more distressing confusion, for rat, cat, pigeon, and dog have stolen the parts of herself laid aside for the night. Even the stray animals desert Corinna in a parodic reversal of the usual community of servants who attend to the dressing ritual. A "dreadful Sight," she frightens even the bashful muse, who retires and leaves her to her private horror.

What we see in comparing Ames's *Folly of Love* and

Swift's "A Beautiful Young Nymph" is that Swift's addition to the tradition, other than a more concrete catalogue, is the sympathy for Corinna's plight that he allows. As John Aden has pointed out, the pathetic element is too strong to be ignored.[20] In the lines "Never did *Covent Garden* boast / So bright a battr'd, strolling Toast," the word "battr'd" surprises us with its hint of compassion. Similarly, other lines at first seduce us to pity her plight. Corinna must be her own physician. She tends to "her Shankers, Issues, running Sores, / Effects of many a sad Disaster" (ll. 30-31). Her dreams are of confinement in prison and a hedge tavern, deportation to the colonies, and capture in *"Fleet-Ditch's* Oozing Brinks" when caught by "Watchmen, Constables and Duns." But the poet intrudes to remind us of the crude reality. Corinna's fancy never flees "from Religious Clubs; / Whose Favour she is sure to find, / Because she pays 'em all in Kind" (ll. 54-56). Her own creator, she must reconstruct herself by morning light with the "Anguish, Toil, and Pain, / Of gath'ring up herself again." But the exposed Corinna is finally the object of our disgust: *"Corinna* in the morning dizen'd, / Who sees, will spew; who smells, be poison'd." The reader can scoff at Ames's lady, but he is tormented by Corinna and forced to contemplate her feelings. The woman is not simply a sexual object or a lusty whore or a deceiver whom we readily flail. She forces our emotional engagement; we cannot remain completely detached. But once her lover has truly perceived her, he can release himself from the madness of love. The harsh mechanical ritual of Corinna's removal of her artificial parts keeps any tendency toward a sentimental portrayal of a whore's lonely night of tortured dreams under tight control, yet Swift displays an understanding for the whore's pains, which is missing in Juvenal and irrelevant in Ovid. Implicit in "A Beautiful Young Nymph" and more explicit in "Strephon and Chloe" and "The Lady's Dressing Room" is Swift's criticism of men who must discover and rediscover, to their surprise, that women are mortal.[21] A parody of the idealization of the sex, the poems insist that women, stripped of their carefully arranged exteriors, are disturbingly common, not goddesses or nymphs, and that a man's sanity depends upon his recognition of that fact.

The boudoir is the place of dressing and undressing; it is also the place where women tend to excretory functions, as Swift reminds us in "The Lady's Dressing Room." Again the scene appears in Ovid's *Remedia Amoris*: "One passion was checked, because the lover, in full train, saw the obscene parts exposed; another, because, when the woman arose from the business of love, the couch was seen to be soiled by shameful marks. You are not in earnest, if any there be whom such things have power to influence: your hearts were kindled by feeble fires" (p. 207). Cupid will attack again, for the true man in love will not let a lady's boudoir dissuade him from pursuing her. The satirist is an uneasy voyeur. The counsel of Ovid continues: "What of him who lurked in hiding while the girl performed her obscenities, and saw what every custom forbids to see? Heaven forfend I should give anyone such counsel! though it may help, 'twere better not to use it" (pp. 208-09). Swift, then, was drawing on classical precedent for presenting shocking scenes from a woman's private closet. The dressing room is divested of its mystique as a place of artistry where a woman creates a self to present to the world. The satirist's art of stripping and revealing reassures men that the boudoir contains nothing they might want to see. If they must see it, they must accept it and forever alter their perception of the sex. Both "A Beautiful Young Nymph" and "The Lady's Dressing Room" seem puzzling at the end—the first because the final lines are completely devoid of pathos, the second because Swift seems to have reversed himself, finding something redemptive in the revelation of the dressing room. The message, for any man who seeks it, is that the boudoir offers a check on lust, a restraint on the madness of passion, and a possiblity of rescuing man from his own irrational fancies.

Swift's point in writing the poems that nauseate their readers is to release men from passion and its attendant madness rather than to reform women's boudoir habits. Swift seeks to destroy the misapprehensions in both sexes which lead to the folly of love. If women create myths for themselves, as they do at the dressing table, they are also subject to the myths men create for them, and that is the origin of Swift's compassion for Corinna. His warning exposes the madness of loving a Corinna and allows us to see the vain imaginings passion brings.

Swift raises serious issues in pointed poems, and unlike Juvenal and native seventeenth-century satirists who contend that the whole sex is without hope of redemption, Swift betrays his faith that women are capable of improvement—they simply fail to exercise the reason God gave them. If Swift hates all of womankind, it seems to be in the same way he detests the whole of mankind and claims to love the individual Peter or Thomas—in this case, the individual Vanessa or Stella. Woman, like man, is not a rational animal, but only *rationis capax.* Thus, while his early poems complain that the ideal woman has vanished into the past, he sets up an androgynous ideal in "Cadenus and Vanessa." While he expresses disgust at women's failure to redeem time, and cautions men against being ensnared by diseased women or their own illusions about the sex in "The Lady's Dressing Room" or "Strephon and Chloe," he also writes poems to Stella in which he presents a positive ideal who is not praised at the expense of her sex. She is, instead, presented as a woman who has wisely made use of what every woman has available to her.

In the poems to Stella he presents the positive ideal against which we can judge the other poems on women.[22] Stella is a female Apollo whose lustrous eyes, splendid wit, dauntless honor, and constant virtue remain stable in the face of fleeting time. Swift suggests in "To Janus on New Year's Day" (1729) that a lady's New Year's gift ought to be a second face turned in retrospection toward her glorious past. The lady, Lady Acheson, indignantly refuses:

> Drown your Morals, Madam cryes;
> I'll have none but forward Eyes:
> Prudes decay'd about may tack,
> Strain their Necks with looking back:

> Give me *Time* when coming on:
> Who regards him when he's gone? [ll. 19-24]

In Stella's last birthday poem (1726/27), Swift shows that
Stella needs no such gift. One of the few virtuous ladies,
Stella is praised for her willingness to look back, and her
strength to look ahead: "For Virtue in her daily Race, /
Like *Janus*, bears a double Face; / Looks back with Joy
where she has gone, / And therefore goes with Courage on"
(ll. 73-76).

On the one hand, Swift cruelly marks the passing of time
for his beloved friend; on the other, he transforms her
mortality, her inevitable physical decay, into an emblem of
his respect and love for her. In the scatological poems, Swift
cautions lovers to look carefully at nymphs in their boudoirs,
yet he boasts of his own inability to see Stella's physical
flaws. His diminishing sight quite naturally parallels her
increasing deterioration:

> But, *Stella* say, what evil Tongue
> Reports you are no longer young?
> That *Time* sits with his Scythe to mow
> Where erst sate *Cupid* with his Bow;
> That half your Locks are turn'd to Grey;
> I'll ne'er believe a Word they say,
> 'Tis true, but let it not be known,
> My Eyes are somewhat dimmish grown;
> For Nature, always in the Right,
> To your Decays adapts my Sight,
> And Wrinkles undistinguish'd pass,
> For I'm asham'd to use a Glass;
> And till I see them with these Eyes,
> Whoever says you have them, lyes. [ll. 35-48]

In collecting and transcribing his poems, Stella produces
order from "this Pile of scatter'd Rhymes" while other
women fall into a scattered heap themselves. Possessed of
healing power, she is a sustainer of life rather than a death-
giving whore. In a compliment describing Stella's birth in

"To Stella, Visiting me in my Sickness" (1720), Swift suggests that she was created to be an androgynous being:

> No: 'Twas for you alone he stole
> The Fire that forms a manly Soul;
> Then to compleat it ev'ry way,
> He molded it with Female Clay:
> To that you owe the nobler Flame.
> To this, the Beauty of your Frame. [ll. 87-92]

Swift, then, is not at all concerned about women's aping men—he seems to encourage women to adopt men's most admirable qualities. He implies that she avoids typical female behavior like hysteria, and he applauds her courage and her willingness to allow her brilliant wit and sense to display themselves. As a woman who tends him in his sickness, she responds to his needs with a rare blend of tenderness and vigor. The Stella of the poems is not praised primarily as the chaste guardian of moral values but as an able, alert companion who delights her friend because of her humanity.[23] His ideal woman, fat, grey, and ill, is decidedly not a lady from romance. Stella's place is on earth with Swift, not in eternity with the angels.

Swift combined the tragic impulse of Juvenal (the attack on marriage) with the comic impulse of Ovid (the attack on romantic illusion), and both with the native tradition; and he shapes a rhetorical stance of complexity and subtlety that has led to widely divergent interpretations of his poems, both in the eighteenth century and now, from the pathological ragings of a misogynist to the studied moralism of a Christian ministering to his deceived flock. Turning away from the traditional Christian dimensions of women as Eve's daughters, Swift pays much less attention than Juvenal to the way women encourage luxury, make men powerless, and contribute to the fall of civilization. Instead he warns both sexes about women's unwillingness to redeem time and women's capacity to bring about men's moral and spiritual demise. For Swift, Stella's values of honor, sense, wit, and friendship are noble goals, and he urges both sexes to seek them. They need not rise above their sex in order to attain the goals—they need only concentrate their energy and attention, in spite of undeniable obstacles, on becoming reasonable creatures.

VII

Enemies and Enviers: Minor Eighteenth-Century Satires

Most late seventeenth-century satires on women censure the whole sex and make few distinctions between good and evil members of the sex. Several eighteenth-century satires indicate the strong influence of Juvenal and Boileau in the later period, but equally strong is a tendency in other eighteenth-century satires to depart from their Restoration antecedents. Joseph Addison and Edward Young were among those who set out to separate themselves from the harsh satiric vein of Juvenal and Boileau, to reform their readers overtly and convincingly, and to offer an object of praise within the satires in the formal verse satire tradition.

Lord Lyttleton's *Advice to a Lady* (1731) is somewhat typical of the milder vein of eighteenth-century satires. The poem does not provide lists of characters, and it is mildly satiric and overtly didactic.[1] Addressed to Belinda in the hope that it "would [her] charms improve, / And form [her] heart to all the arts of love," it acknowledges that she already displays considerable talent in these areas. Though Lord Lyttleton recites the usual charges against the sex (that women make few friends, that their highest goal is beauty), he also provides instruction in wit, virtue, love, and marriage. There is more counsel than reproach in the poet's words: "Seek to be good, but aim not to be great: / A woman's

noblest station is retreat: / Her fairest virtues fly from public
sight, / Domestic worth, that shuns too strong a light."

Female Chastity (1735) and *Swift's Vision* (1757)[2] are
both among the antifeminist diatribes that cite Juvenal and
Boileau as precedents. Both begin with the familiar disclaimer
that their satires are not intended to criticize particular living
women or the entire sex. The poet in *Female Chastity* contends, "Nevertheless, I presume the most Deserving of
Womankind, have no Cause of Distast; not only as They are
above Censure, and may therefore bid Defyance to It; but
because an Explod[ing of?] the Degenerate, is the best Foil,
to render opposite Excellence, the more distinguishably
eminent!" And in *Swift's Vision,* the advertisement to the
reader states, "The Author is above all Things sollicitous, that
every Body shou'd know, and he seriously protests that they
may also believe, the following POEM is altogether general.
Nor can he apprehend that even the Characters of *Laura,
Mira, and Drusa,* will bear a particular Application, whilst the
World abounds with Myriads of such Characters." To claim
the satire is general, then, is the conventional disclaimer that
no living women should see themselves in the mirror of the
satire.

The anonymous poet of *Female Chastity* places the poem
in the tradition of Juvenal and Boileau, and "even the polite
and elegant Virgil's *varium, et mutabile, semper Femina* is, I
think as Sharp an Invective against the female Sex, as can be
compriz'd in so small a Compass" (p. 3). Like Juvenal's or
Boileau's satires, the poem includes no paragon and its tone is
vindictive, but the poem is more overtly moral in its intention than are its precedessors. After the usual charges against
women as deceivers, a fop speaks in behalf of the sex. His
praise has considerable double meaning since, for example, he
suggests that the famed Lucretia really lusted after her rapist.
Women only complain about attacks on their chastity if the
men are inadequate:

> Had her [Lucretia's] plump Beings been fill'd with
> vig'rous Fire,

And had the Gallant well-suited her Desire;
Had She (the Deed committed) still been sure,
Her Reputation wou'd no Blot endure;
The resolute, the celebrated Bride,
Had kill'd Herself, before She had deny'd! [p. 7]

The poet emphasizes women's insatiable lust by using the
metaphor of trade (familiar to readers of Restoration satire),
that they are ports which can take in any ship. They convert
the church into a marketplace "And make the House of God,
the Devil's Exchange." Even ancient British nuns found ways
to trade with "the hooded monk" and "cowled Friar"
though "free Commerce" with the larger world was pro-
hibited. The poem concludes with an impassioned warning to
men: if they learn what women really are they will free themselves from the yoke of women. Men will regain their lost
power only if they, like skilled adventurers, steer away from
rocks and sand and determine their course well in advance.
Female Chastity is also unlike its predecessors in that it never warns specifically against marriage, only against the failure
of chastity, and it serves to warn men against women's lust
and deceit.

Swift's Vision is more mildly antifeminist. It claims to be a
response to Pope's "Epistle to a Lady": The deities

Had once with great Resentment heard
Of a despotick hump-back'd Bard,
Who took upon him to declare
A strange Opinion of the Fair;
Affirming of them, great and small,
"Most have no Characters at all:"
From whence each Goddess cou'd foresee
Subversion of her Deity. [p. 6]

The junto of goddesses take affront at the charges levelled
against women, and they ask Swift to contradict Pope. In
their plea they argue that women must at least be allowed
characters, though the descriptions are comic:

> Cow'd *Drusa,* having no Pretence
> To Wit, to Learning, or to Sense,
> As much on Frippery presume,
> On gaudy Silks and Knots of Bloom,
> As if she were acquainted well
> With Things, beyond what we can tell? [p. 10]

Thus the goddesses and their arguments become the object of satire. Their debate, which altruistically defends the sex, is, of course, self-serving. In spite of Pope's decree, women "must, they will have characters." The poet concludes by pleading muteness in the face of the glorious few whom Pope excepted from his condemnation: "But still a noble Few there are, / With Virtues, like themselves, most rare. / *By Pope* excepted from the Throng, / Above the Reach of Pen or Tongue" (p. 14). The poem concludes with irony. Swift accepts their claim and shows that women have characters—though not necessarily good ones: "He grants them all he can impart, / What Wit inspires and flows from Art, / Yet not the Tenth of their Desert" (p. 15).

When Joseph Addison translated an early Greek anti-feminist creation story in *Spectator* No. 209 (30 October 1711), he concluded the paper by distinguishing himself from the ancients and insisting on the efficacy of satire:

As the Poet has shewn a great Penetration in this Diversity of Female Characters, he has avoided the Fault which *Juvenal* and Monsieur *Boileau* are guilty of, the former in his Sixth, and the other in his last Satyr, where they endeavoured to expose the Sex in general, without doing Justice to the valuable Part of it. . . . What Vice or Frailty can a Discourse correct, which censures the whole Species alike, and endeavours to shew by some Superficial Strokes of Wit, that Brutes are the more excellent Creatures of the two? A Satyr should expose nothing but what is corrigible, and make a due Discrimination between those who are, and those who are not, the proper Objects of it.[3]

The gentler satiric spirit characterizes much eighteenth-century writing on women, including that of Addison, Steele, and many minor satirists. Richard Steele, Addison's friend and collaborator, paid considerable attention to the social roles of women in his *Spectator*. As Rae Blanchard has pointed out, Steele sought to reform women by heightening their self-respect.[4] He presents large numbers of unappealing female characters as negative examples in his periodical essays, but he contrasts virtuous women to the wanton, affected women, and violent women to the gentle. And in No. 432 (16 July 1712) his "correspondent" writes that he deplores general satires of any kind: "I always hated Satyrs against Woman, and Satyrs against Man."[5] It is significant, then, that when Addison chose to translate a satire against women, he chose Semonides' version of the creation story (seventh century B.C.) as derived from Hesiod (eighth century B.C.)[6] because Semonides, unlike Juvenal, Boileau, or Restoration satirists, introduced an ideal woman, a paragon against which to judge the other women. The Semonides fragment was also known to seventeenth- and early eighteenth-century readers from William Walsh's *Dialogue Concerning Women*. There "Misogynes," using the fragment as historical evidence to bolster his argument, ignores the implication that one good woman may give the lie to women's inherent inferiority. He says, "There is a Story also of this *Simonides,* that being askt about a Wife, he said, she was the Shipwreck of Man, the Tempest of a House, the Disturber of Rest, the Prison of Life, a sumptuous conflict, a Beast in Company, a necessary Evil."[7] In the original version, Semonides follows the second of two creation stories told by Hesiod, and probably derived from folk tales, to show that Zeus created woman to curse mankind. The Greek fragment contains 115 lines which describe nine kinds of unappealing women who are created as men's plague. Zeus created seven women from animals and two from the elements of earth and sea. A tenth woman who, like a bee, is a good wife, is industrious and virtuous. Semonides allots almost as much space to the paragon (93 lines) as to the unappealing women (115 lines). The concluding diatribe against women is brief but pointed (22 lines).

Typical of Addison's and Steele's portrayal of women in extremes in the *Spectator* is the Greek motto from Semonides that introduces *Spectator* No. 209: "A man cannot possess anything that is better than a good Woman, nor anything that is worse than a bad one." Addison justifies the inclusion of the satiric piece on moral grounds; comparing eighteenth-century women to women of an earlier age will "shame us out of any particular Vice, or animate us to any particular Virtue ... and to rectifie that Narrowness of Temper which inclines us to think amiss of those who differ from our selves." Semonides' satire is instructive. After claiming to have followed the original very closely, Addison apologizes for the indecency of the language, but readers of Restoration satires would find his translation exceedingly decorous in comparison to the violent obscenities hurled by the seventeenth-century pamphleteers. Further, Addison apologizes in accordance with convention and dissociates most of the sex from Semonides' strictures. The satire "affects only some of the lower part of the Sex, and not those who have been refined by a Polite Education, which was not so common in the Age of this Poet."

Addison provides an entertaining translation of Semonides' list of women who were formed from the souls of animals and the elements, and he places appropriate emphasis on the domestic qualities of the paragon, the tenth woman who "is altogether faultless and unblameable." Faithful to her husband, a good mother, she rises above her sex and avoids wasting time with loose women. In short, she "is the best Wife that Jupiter can bestow on Man." Addison concludes with a reiteration of the extremes women can represent and the instructive nature of satire. What is most interesting, however, is that Addison omits Semonides' final censure of the sex, consisting of twenty-two lines, and seems unaware of its existence. The unflinching condemnation of the sex which he congratulates Semonides on avoiding is, in fact, an important part of the original Greek fragment. After having praised the tenth species of woman, "full of Vertue and Prudence," the original Semonides fragment turns to violent satires against wives, with a lengthy tabulation of failures in virtue. Such a progression seems to work against the conventions of formal verse satire, in which the object of praise gains the emphasis which comes naturally from concluding the work. Semonides provides the paragon, but then he returns to a description of women as the plague Zeus created to torment men:

> The man who lives with a woman never goes through all his day in cheerfulness. . . . Just when a man most wishes to enjoy himself at home, through the dispensation of a god or the kindness of a man, she finds a way of finding fault with him and lifts her crest for battle. Yes, where there is a woman, men cannot even give hearty entertainment to a guest who has come to the house; and the very woman who seems most respectable is the one who turns out guilty of the worst atrocity. . . . Yes, this is the greatest plague Zeus has made, and he has bound us to them with a fetter that cannot be broken. Because of this some have gone to Hades fighting for a woman. . . .[8]

This is a distinctly Juvenalian tone, and it makes Addison's requirement that satire should distinguish its particular objects from the species inapplicable to the Semonides fragment he chose to translate. For whatever reason, Addison did not include the condemnation of the sex. Perhaps the translation he used (possibly Walsh's) did not include it or perhaps he willfully misconstrued the original, but in any case, Addison's ideas on the moral instructiveness of satire and the inclusion of a paragon could not be applied to Juvenal, Boileau, or Restoration satires on women. His essay indicates the beginnings of a willingness, even a compulsion, to include an ideal within the structure of the satire. With the inclusion of an ideal, the myth of the Restoration woman is threatened. An object of praise within the satire begins to create tensions within the satires on women that cannot be easily resolved. Those tensions are apparent in other minor eighteenth-century satires that follow the Hesiod/Semonides creation tale, as well as in satires by Edward Young and others.[9]

In an anonymous poem, *The Creation of Women* (1725), the author notes that he follows Addison's *Spectator* No. 209 in his translation of Semonides, but in the Argument he extends Addison's intention by including examples of equally offensive males, so that "the Ladies will think themselves reveng'd for the Affronts cast upon them by the unmannerly Grecian," and he concludes with a long tribute to an ideal virtuous woman: "'Midst these *Clarissa,* eminently bright, / Shall with ten thousand Beauties wound the Sight; / Contending Rivals shall her Charms declare, / And in sweet Numbers eternize the Fair."[10]

In *Hesiod: or, the Rise of Woman* (1755), Thomas Parnell writes a poetic version of Hesiod's creation story without allusion to Semonides, but the latter's influence remains. Pandora, the woman created from each god's particular gift, encompasses the charms and the flaws of all women. Prometheus molds the frame, Vulcan the shape, Juno the pride and fancy, Minerva the art of dress, Hermes the contriving, and Apollo the wit and flattery. The virgins provide a soft sweet voice, the Graces the tools for artifice, and Flora flowers. Each god or goddess does not provide something distinctly different, and the creation is somewhat repetitious. Pandora, exemplifying the typical traits of women, wastes time, seeks power, is inconstant and falsely bright. She of course entices man to yield to her beauty and power, and the result is the release of evil forces from the box she carries. Only a few women rise above the tendencies of their sex in the poem: "Ye fair offended, hear your friend relate / What heavy judgment prov'd the writer's fate, / Tho' when it happen'd, no relation clears, / 'Tis thought in five, or five and twenty years."[11] The moral of this lightly satirical classical version of creation is that women, from the day of their creation, have been dangerous to men.

At first it seems rather surprising that one of the few eighteenth-century English imitations of Boileau's satire *Contre les femmes* was penned by Lady Mary Wortley Montagu when she accompanied her husband, the ambassa-

dor to Turkey, to Constantinople (1717-18). The recent
editor of Lady Mary's poem, Isobel Grundy, remarks in a
headnote to the satire that "as an attack on women, it stands
out oddly among her works."[12] During her Turkish sojourn
Lady Mary astutely observed Turkish women and in her
letters remarked on their apparent freedom in the bagnio.
Apparently in her early years Lady Mary accepted the idea,
so pervasive in the satires cited in these pages, that to scorn
other women was to enhance her own worth. Her early
feminism insists on drawing distinctions between herself and
most other women. During the same period of time that she
was writing her imitation of Boileau, she wrote regularly on
feminist topics, for she was much aware that "'women are
treated in Turkey as something between beasts and men,' and
possess an inferior order of souls."[13] It was not until many
years later that she specifically condemned satires against
women because they undermined women's faith in their own
abilities. In 1738 she wrote, "If I was a divine I would re-
member that in their first Creation they were designd a Help
for the other Sex, and nothing was ever made incapable of
the end of its Creation. 'Tis true the first Lady had so little
experience that she hearkend to the persuasions of an Impertinent Dangler; and if you mind . . . he succeeded by per-
suadeing her that she was not so wise as she should be and I
own I suspect something like this device under the raillerys
that are so freely apply'd to the Fair Sex."[14]

The question remains: Why did Lady Mary write such a
satire, the very breed of satire she condemned in later years?
Apparently her feminism became consistent only in her
middle age.[15] Various letters from her youth reveal her
understandable tendency to count herself among the fortunate few who have risen above her sex. She writes to Wortley
in 1710, "I [am] so far from the usual vanity of [my] sex, as
not to expect any su[ch jus]tice upon my account. I suppose this will pass for Affectation, but I know there may be a
Woman uninterested and artlesse."[16] She generalizes about
women's follies—their insincerity, their love of inflicting pain,
their love of trifles. And the next year she assures him, "I am
not one of those foolish vain Women [who] think nothing so

Impor[tant] as themselves." Again she argues, "I am not of the Number of those Women that have the Opinion of their persons Mr. Bayes had of his Play, that tis the touchstone of sense, and they are to frame their Judgment of people's understandings according to what they think of them . . . I have not the usual Pride of my Sex," and "I shall make none of the complaints another Woman would do" for "There are not manny Women that would so far mistrust their own power of pleasing."[17]

As a young woman Lady Mary clearly pursued an independent path and shaped her character without feminine models, but she simultaneously defended herself from the inevitable charges against her sex that she rightly anticipated. After having shown her translation of Epictetus to Bishop Burnet, she carefully avoids being stereotyped as the character she portrays in her satires: "There is hardly a character in the World more despicable or more liable to universal ridicule than that of a Learned Woman. Them words imply, according to the receiv'd sense, a tatling, impertinent, vain, and Conceited Creature." But she hastens to add, "I am not now arguing for an Equality for the 2 Sexes; I do not doubt God and Nature has thrown us into an Inferior Rank."[18] To rebel against her God-ordained subordinate and obedient role would encourage disorder and atheism, just as in her satiric portrait the learned lady is an "odious Character":

> The Learned She, who makes her wise remarks
> On Whiston's Lectures or on Dr Clark's,
> And quite dispiseing mean Domestic Cares
> Only regards the motions of the Stars. [ll. 148-51]
>
> . . . .
>
> Boldly derideing Superstitious fear,
> Raillys the mysterys she should revere,
> Mistakeing what she cannot comprehend
> In downright Atheism her Studys end. [ll. 156-59]

In fact, her epistolary exchanges with Wortley rest on the premise that her behavior must not be identified with that of most women. Only later, after years of being satirized herself as a learned lady, did she insist on sexual equality: "(If I dare say it) that Nature has not plac'd us in a inferior Rank to Men, no more than the Females of other Animals, where we see no distinction of capacity, thô I am persuaded if there was a Common-wealth of rational Horses (as Doctor Swift has suppos'd) it would be an established maxim amongst them that a mare could not be taught to pace."[19]

Certainly the fact that Lady Mary expressed only a limited feminist consciousness as a young woman in Turkey could account for her willingness to translate Boileau's Satire X, *Contre les femmes*.[20] The original, like Montagu's imitation, is both an argument against marriage and a satire on women. Boileau's satire occasioned a battle, with attacks by Bossuet, Renard, and Perrault, among others. Again, the kinds of responses suggest that his work was seen primarily as an attack on marriage, like Juvenal's Sixth Satire, rather than as an attack on the sex. The cynicism concerning marriage in the poem is consistent with a fragment of Lady Mary's autobiography that remains, in which she styles herself a precocious romantic heroine, the daughter of a duke. Unlike other girls, she "never thought of marriage but as a Bond that was to subject her to a Master, and she dreaded an Engagement of that sort."[21] The heroine prefers the company of Virgil and Horace to that of men. Through the intrigue of her suitor and her chambermaid, she is betrothed to Sebastian with her own consent. In the fragment, the tone cynically mocks romance in life and literature.

Much longer than Montagu's version, the Boileau original opens with a statement in which the poet disavows any general condemnation of women and argues for his moral intention. He even solicits the approval of good women in the condemnation of their sex. Lady Mary omits Boileau's opening apology and moves immediately to a dialogue between an adviser and a man, "Sated with Pleasure," who seeks a marriage partner. He wants a wife to comfort him in his declining years, to trick his "Greedy heirs," to procreate, to seek happiness, and to provide legal sanction for his sexual appetite. The introductory argument that marriage has its pleasures is omitted from Montagu, as are the references to archetypal faithful wives and cuckolded husbands. Both the original and its imitation emphasize how important the right choice of wife can be. Boileau allots considerable space to a description of the vulnerability and loneliness of the alternative life, bachelorhood. But Lady Mary's version is really only a fragment of a poem, and moves directly to the most memorable portions of the original, the catalogue of undesirable wives, such as the gaming spendthrift, the parsimonious manager, and the coquettish virgin. The sense of moral awareness deepens in Lady Mary's fragment, from the woman whose "artless Innocence" is corrupted by the town, to the woman who knowingly exerts her power to create domestic disharmony, "The House a Scene of strong perpetual Noise, / The Servants' Curses or the Children's Cries" (ll. 123-24). Even worse is the jealous wife who skulks about town in search of her husband's lovers:

> Then is the time to know the Sexes Fire,
> What vengeance Vain Suspicion can inspire,
> In every Street you meet her watchfull Spies
> And oft her selfe mobd in some odd Disguise
> With Thunder on her Tongue and Light'ning in her
> Eyes. [ll. 125-31]

Three very successful, detailed, and clever portraits conclude the fragment—"a sickly fair," the "Learned She" and a politician. Lady Mary mocks the female politician more for her belief in her own power than for her potential to rule the world. The female busybody actively solicits power:

> The Politician whose fantastic Zeal
> Impairs her Health to mind the Public weal,
> Makes grave Reflections on the weekly Lies,
> Reads all the Pamphlets Grubstreet can devise,

Even at her Tea instead of female Chat
With matchiavilian Art reforms the State. [ll. 162-67]

But here Montagu's imitation ends abruptly, while
Boileau's Satire X continues at great length with an exhaustive list of stereotypic women and insists at the conclusion
that no woman can escape her sex's faults. Alcippe, the
groom-to-be, mocks the extremity of the poet's argument
and maintains that his wife will avoid the faults that are
satirized. But marriage is a permanent state, the narrator reminds Alcippe, and because the courts favor women, Alcippe
ought not take such a poor risk. Neither the original nor
Lady Mary's imitation proposes any alternatives to the general condemnation of the sex. Yet in a poem written in 1724
but unpublished in her lifetime, "Epistle from Mrs. Y[onge]
to her Husband," Montagu criticizes marriage because of the
inevitable suffering wives with adulterous husbands must
undergo. In other words, her own views shifted to sympa-
thize with married women rather than with married men:

From whence is this unjust Distinction grown?
Are we not form'd with Passions like your own?
Nature with equal Fire our Souls endu'd,
Our Minds as Haughty, and as warm our blood,
O're the wide World your pleasures you persue,
The Change is justify'd by something new;
But we must sigh in Silence—and be true.[22] [ll. 25-31]

She is remarkable in her open acknowledgment of women's
sexuality, her awareness of the double standard, and her
sympathy with women's social situation.

Acutely aware of the subtleties of "the sneer of affected
Admiration," Lady Mary might well have found Edward
Young's satires on women among those she warned women
against when she said, "Begin then Ladies by paying those
Authors with Scorn and contempt who with the sneer of
affected Admiration would throw you below the Dignity of
the Human Species."[23] Many of the conflicting impulses in

satires against women that this chapter has elucidated come
into play in Young's satires on women. Young (1683-1765)
makes clear in his preface to *Love of Fame, the Universal
Passion* (1725-28) that his poetic voice prefers laughing,
general satire to vituperation, the comic to the tragic. He
does not intend "the least malevolence to any particular
person."[24] Satire, he acknowledges, may be ineffectual, and
the passion that is most appropriate to men's folly is "to
smile at it, and turn it into ridicule." Though he places himself in the tradition of Boileau and Juvenal, he is more accurate when he distinguishes himself from them: "But though I
comparatively condemn Juvenal, [in relation to Horace] in
part of the sixth satire (where the occasion most required it),
I endeavored to touch on his manner; but was forced to quit
it soon, as disagreeable to the writer, and reader too. Boileau
has joined both the Roman satirists with great success; but
has too much of Juvenal in his very serious satire on woman,
which should have been the gayest of all."

Young begins with a claim that the satires actually honor
the sex: "The sex we honour, tho' their faults we blame; /
Nay, thank their faults for such a fruitful theme: / A theme,
fair—! doubly kind to me, / Since satirizing those is praising
thee." The satire is a loosely structured series of negative
examples, interspersed with miniature generalized moral
essays and alternative positive portraits of ideal women. The
ostensible unifying factor is women's love of fame: women,
like the men in earlier portions of *Love of Fame,* are ambi-
tious in their own lesser sphere. Satire V opens with lines
from Milton describing Eve's love of fame: "O fairest of
creation! . . . How art thou lost!" In Juvenal and Boileau, the
various portraits of undesirables are held together by a frame
of a dialogue between a man who seeks a bride and his
counselor against marriage. Such a frame does not appear in
Young; his purpose is to reform women rather than to
frighten men.

Young's intention seems to be, then, to unite the impulses
of ridicule and reform, to chastise women severely, and yet
to offer them models for reformation. Howard Weinbrot
argues fully and convincingly that Young does not under-

stand that the malicious tragic impulse of the portraits of reprobate women cannot be easily and comically resolved by an appeal to the simple goodness of the women.[25] It is as if Young negates his tragic vision with a quick glance at the comic. Weinbrot is quite right in recognizing the conflicting impulses within the poem; I would add that the problems in the poem arise as much from the history of satires on women—a problem Addison begged by omitting part of the Semonides fragment, a question Swift avoided by keeping the ideal separate and withdrawn from his satires on women, and that Pope resolved by creating enormous ambiguity within the individual portraits of women in "Epistle to a Lady." Young was unable to evoke that complexity within any of the individual portraits; instead it is created in an artificial manner with interjections of moral essays between the portraits of reprobate women. This technique makes for confusion and irritation rather than complexity and moral ambiguity.

Young uses familiar examples of undesirable women—the learned lady, the Amazon, the astronomer, the prudish coquette, the affected devout—to insist on his theme that women should be kind, virtuous, calm, and restrained rather than jealous for fame. Women should create harmony, and their happiness, as well as the happiness of men, depends on their ability to accept their lesser and quieter sphere with grace. Examples of women who overcome the natural tendencies of their sex, as well as pieces of moral wisdom, are interjected between the series of portraits of reprobate women. This technique repeatedly interrupts the force of the satire and threatens the myth of women created in the portraits. The rhythm of the piece jolts the reader as he seeks the ideal among the reprobates.

Satire V begins, for example, with a catalogue of vain women. Clarinda attempts to be an all-conquering hero, Zara seeks religious glory, Xantippe affects great wisdom: "Is't not enough plagues, wars, and famines, rise / To lash our crimes, but must our wives be wise?" This introduces a brief moral essay on the plagues women can create, an essay which concludes with a description of the tenderness and calm a proper woman can create: "How have I seen a gentle nymph draw nigh, / Peace in her air, persuasion in her eye; / Victorious tenderness! it all o'ercame, / Husbands look'd mild, and savages grew tame." Then again the satiric impulse dominates the poem as Young describes women's unrestrained appetites—Delia's for riding, Daphne's for learning, Sempronia's for possessions. They all contrast to Stella, who proves that beauty and intelligence can be united: "O no: see Stella; her eyes shine as bright / As if her tongue was never in the right; / And yet what real learning, judgment, fire! / She seems inspir'd, and can herself inspire."

Another series of women madly pursue the elusive pleasure their imaginations create in order for the poet to demonstrate how empty such pleasures can be. Lemira, for example, quickly forgets her illness when offered the opportunity to dance: "For want—but not of health, are ladies ill; / And tickets cure beyond the doctor's pill." The next series presents women who spoil their own happiness—Amelia, whose disputes over works by D'Urfey and Bunyan destroy her marriage; Phoebe, who longs for the past or future; Flavia, who falls into despair because of her lover's rejection. Among the other numerous malcontents are Rosalinda, a languid portrait of impotence; Thalestris, the Amazon who shamelessly imitates men; and Lyce, a *memento mori* who plans new conquests on her husband's tomb: "Gay rainbow silks her mellow charms infold, / And nought of Lyce but herself is old / Her grizzled locks assume a smirking grace, / And art has levell'd her deep-furrow'd face."

The moral advice and the ideal women forwarded, like the portraits of undesirables, are often redundant as the weight of the satire shifts toward examples of virtue. It is difficult, for example, to take a satire against famed women seriously when the ideal women are so famous their names cannot be revealed:[26]

> To —— turn; she never took the height
> Of Saturn, yet is ever in the right.
> She strikes each point with native force of mind,
> While puzzled learning blunders far behind,

> Graceful to sight, and elegant to thought,
> The great are vanquish'd and the wise are taught.

The portrait is undistinguished, and a reader accustomed to
watching for the inconsistencies in the undesirable women's
characters finds himself having to read extraordinarily closely
in order to be certain Young intends no irony in lines such as
"Sincere, and warm, with zeal well understood, / She takes a
novel pride in doing good." Tributes to "high-born Anna"
and to "prudent Portia" conclude Satire V. Portia, the opposite of the *memento mori,* becomes a symbol for graceful—
even jubilant—acceptance of death. As joy departs with her
advancing age, she calls for death. Like Pope, Young sympathizes with his satiric victim. The poem concludes with a
sentimental concern for Portia's orphaned daughters, and the
poet offers advice which sympathizes with the plight of
unprotected women: "Most hard! in pleasing your chief glory
lies; / And yet from pleasing your chief dangers rise: / Then
please the best; and know, for men of sense / Your strongest
charms are native innocence."

Satire VI does not offer enough variation to justify a
second satire. It is dedicated to Lady Elizabeth Germain,
who, because she takes Young's advice in Satire V, "to shine
unknown," will be properly embarrassed by his public praise.
The satire begins with Lavinia's affected religion and Drusa's
affected sensuality. Young then explores some specific
women's relationships to men. Flavia, Amasia, Abra, and
Lucia exemplify various states from unmarried piety to
marriage to a fool. Women tease men and create pain for
them: "For pleasure form'd, perversely some believe, / To
make themselves important, men must grieve. / Lesbia the
fair, to fire her jealous lord, / Pretends, the fop she laughs at,
is ador'd." Similarly, Mira and Melania cause disquietude to
their lovers. Melania, who "never thinks her lover pays his
due," serves as a transition in a miniature lecture on the
transience of beauty. Aspasia too, though beautiful, finds
considerable distress in her life and becomes the occasion for
another digression on the frailty of life. After a list of women
who seek amusements, Young speaks of the inequity with

which the world bestows fame. Here too the moral digressions overwhelm the characters. They stress woman's affectation, the relationship between beauty and virtue, the importance of living in the present, the difficulties of achieving success in a perverted age, and the perils of gaming.

When the poet lectures on the ways in which money is insufficient for happiness, he seems to be carried away with the didacticism, and he calls himself up short to return to blame:

> But some, great souls! and touch'd with warmth
>   divine,
> Give gold a price, and teach its beams to shine.
> All hoarded treasures they repute a load;
> Nor think their wealth their own, till well bestow'd
> Grand reservoirs of public happiness,
> Through secret streams diffusively they bless;
> . . . .
> But satire is my task; and these destroy
> Her gloomy province, and malignant joy.
> Help me, ye misers, help me to complain,
> And blast our common enemy, Germain:
> But our invectives must despair success;
> For next to praise, she values nothing less.

Young calls on Juvenal to launch the more violent satiric attack he finds himself avoiding, and he creates a world of unmitigated evil. The satire, which has gently alternated from a few reprobate women to a lovely virtuous woman and back to undesirables, suddenly creates deepening moral awareness:

> Such griping av'rice, such profuse expense;
> Such dead devotion, such a zeal for crimes;
> Such licens'd ill, such masquerading times;
> Such venal faith, such misapplied applause;
> Such flatter'd guilt, and such inverted laws;
> Such dissolution through the whole I find,
> 'Tis not a world, but chaos of mankind.

This world view implies that no alternative is available, and
the reader finds himself confused as to where the many
attractive prudent women Young has described in earlier
portions of Satires V and VI may be found. Juvenal's Sixth
Satire argues that the ideal woman is *rara avis in terris*.
Young suggests that such ideal women are numerous, and
thus the tragic vision of the Juvenalian section seems out of
place. Certainly the turn to Juvenalian satire is inconsistent
with the tone of the earlier portions of the poem. At the
same time, the ideal woman, Queen Caroline, is not a threat
to the myth of satires on women because her portrait is
neither credible nor detailed: "Midst empire's charms, how
Carolina's heart / Glows with the love of virtue, and of art! /
Her favour is diffus'd to that degree, / Excess of goodness! it
has dawn'd on me."[27] Young compares her to a prelapsarian
Eve, a very unsuccessful comparison, for after having read the
list of women who readily fall to temptation, and being fully
cognizant of a satiric tradition in which Eve is the prototype
of the worst of all deceitful sinning women, the reader
cannot help questioning what this ideal woman would do
when faced with temptation, though Young certainly seems
unaware of the implication:

> Thus the majestic mother of mankind,
> To her own charms most amiably blind,
> On the green margin innocently stood,
> And gaz'd indulgent on the crystal flood;
> Survey'd the stranger in the painted wave,
> And, smiling, prais'd the beauties which she gave.

Even if the Juvenalian section and the concluding ideal
were omitted, the satire would fail. It is too repetitious and it
lacks the ambiguity that delights the reader who expects wit
with the attack. Young cannot have it both ways. Young's
including the Juvenalian attacks suggests that he knew his
audience might still expect reference to his more violent
predecessors, but he could not move beyond the immediate
history of satires on women to create the extraordinary

combination of witty satiric attack and stunning portrayal of an ideal woman that we find in Pope's "Epistle to a Lady."

It may be that by the mid-eighteenth century, the image of the ideal woman, virtuous and chaste, largely replaced the satiric myth of whore, infidel, and Amazon in literature. Such a paragon constitutes a new myth, one of a desexualized upholder of the social, domestic, and religious order.[28] Yet the countercurrent (as in the direct translations of Juvenal and Boileau) must have continued to persist as well, for in *The Nonsense of Common-Sense,* Mary Wortley Montagu, writing anonymously, deplores the current literary practice "of treating the weaker sex with a contempt, which has a very bad Influence on their conduct."[29] She adds that there is "hardly one Man in ten but fancys he has one reason or other, to curse some of the Sex most heartily." The literary tradition of Juvenal begins to become more bland with the inclusion of a woman who manages to overcome the inherent limitations of her sex and to rise in stature above a woman. The ambiguity of satire allows for the seventeenth-century possibility, according to the Juvenalian tradition, that no woman can be redeemed—that even a *rara avis* will disgust a man by her affectations of perfection; at the same time, the early and mid-eighteenth century set forth the alternative possibility that the obedient wife, chaste and good, may exist on this earth. There is always the subtle undertone, however, implying that such women, the guardians of moral values, can exist only in the fiction of satire, for they are more than human, more like angels than women. The saint, the moral superior of her would-be seducer—unlike Swift's Stella but exemplified in Richardson's Clarissa—is exquisitely perfect, too perfect for life on this earth.

VIII

"The Glory, Jest, and Riddle of the Town": Women in Pope's Poetry

Alexander Pope, like Young, avoids the explicit scatological humor of Restoration antifeminism and Swift's early eighteenth-century version of it. Pope's poems about women project his compelling interest in and his shrewd assessment of women's predicament. His poetry on women resounds with themes familiar to readers of antifeminist satires. Pope's women exhibit universal characteristics of inconstancy, pride, and self-love—in short, they are prudes or coquettes. It has often been pointed out, however, that Pope seems to reveal an unusual awareness of the control that custom and tradition have over women's lives, while he encourages women to act as models of good humor and good sense in spite of their unavoidable difficulties. He urges Belinda in "The Rape of the Lock" toward a new definition of female heroism, and even his sharpest criticisms of the sex in "Epistle to a Lady" portray his awareness that women's choices were few and the range of virtuous experiences much limited by eighteenth-century society. The mock-heroic "Rape of the Lock" teases Belinda while it displays her entrapment in the rigid rules of courtship, and the satiric "Epistle to a Lady" asserts that most women have no characters, while it provides an example of one woman who succeeds in establishing a stable identity. Certainly Pope knew the antifeminist tradition, and "Rape of the Lock" as well as "Epistle to a Lady" were long seen as eighteenth-century additions to that tradition.

Critics have thoroughly explored the rich contextual history of "The Rape of the Lock" from the most obvious indebtedness to Virgil, Homer, Ovid, Spenser, and Milton, to the more obscure references to William Dapier's *Dryades,* Cowley's *Davideis,* Le Bossu's *Traité du Poème Epique,* and Garth's *Dispensary.*[1] Also important for the context of the poem, though not finally as significant as classical precedents, are commonplace assumptions about women which may be derived from the native English tradition. "Rape of the Lock," like "Epistle to a Lady," opens with an apology that is more a commonplace than has previously been assumed. In the introductory letter to Mrs. Arabella Fermor, Pope argues that poem is "intended only to divert a few young Ladies, who have good Sense and good Humour enough, to laugh not only at their Sex's little unguarded Follies, but at their own."[2] Yet he then feels he must explain the machinery of the sylphs and gnomes to Arabella, and mockingly says he must explicate some hard words, for the fair sex confines its reading to novels. He goes on to insist that the characters bear no similarity to living models: "The Human Persons are as Fictitious as the Airy ones; and the Character of *Belinda,* as it is now manag'd, resembles You in nothing but in Beauty." Of course, we know that Pope intends for us to recognize Arabella Fermor in Belinda, and the disclaimer is simply a polite and lighthearted release of Pope from responsibility for satiric applications of his poetic words.

Such disclaimers have numerous precedents in the history of satires on women. Dryden, of course, absolves himself of responsibility for Juvenal's Sixth Satire by claiming that no Englishwomen fit the Roman's description. In addition, the author of the virulent *A Satyr Upon Old Maids* (1713) offers an unconvincing disclaimer in a postscript: "We expect the foregoing *Satyr* should pass under the like Acceptation with most *General Rules,* which are not free from some *Exceptions;* being well assur'd there be some who continue *Maids* to *Old Age,* through Choice, on *prudent* or pious *Considera-*

ations; who deserve all the Encomiums can be merited by the *Best* of their *Sex*."[3]

William Walsh in *Dialogue Concerning Women* comments that "The Dispute is not whether there have been any Ill Women in the world, but whether there are not more Good."[4] Similarly, in a harsh satire, *The Art of Knowing Women,* translated from French, the author makes reference to his desire to exclude some women from condemnation: "Thank God, I can still name *some* Ladies among us who are shining Patterns of the most sublime Virtue Human Nature can attain to." And he explicitly relieves himself of responsibility for identifying specific living persons: "I must say one Word more on a very ticklish Point. It will doubtless be fancied that I have particular Persons in view under the fictitious Names I have made use of; but, I protest upon the *Word* of a *Gentleman,* that my Intention was only to make *War* upon *Vice* in general. Let any who shall find their own Picture drawn, only blame themselves, and strive to become Copies of more amiable Originals."[5] Most of the satirists claim that their satire is aimed at no particular victim. Even in Boileau's rather mild Tenth Satire against women he indicates that satire should make women his most avid readers rather than being offended by it.[6] The disclaimers in any poem on women may probably be discounted. Of course, no satirist, from the angriest Restoration verse writer to the gentlest eighteenth-century satirist, wished to be identified as a misogynist, a universal hater of the sex. None wished to state that all women are evil. None wished to argue that there were not exceptions to the rules.

In both "The Rape of the Lock" and "Epistle to a Lady," other themes and conventions appear. In both, women divide themselves into prudes and coquettes; they are inconstant and changeable; they pursue pleasure and power; they worship themselves at the expense of others. In both, the imagery of light contrasts the blinding brilliance of the sun with the softer and more proper reflection of the moon. Both poems fleetingly suggest that women are the victims of custom and form—that their lapses from decorous behavior originate in inadequate education, but the "Epistle" clearly

discourages bold displays of learning or wit. Neither poem
arouses much sympathy for the deposed and thwarted male
sex, while both argue vigorously for the value of generous
good humor and good sense. Neither of the poems is finally
misogynist, but each is ambiguous and complex in its use of
eighteenth-century conventions and commonplaces about the
sex.

Two of the most common conventions of the satiric tradition appear in the first canto of "The Rape of the Lock."
Belinda's dressing at her mirror, both goddess and priestess
at her own worship, takes on new significance when seen
in the context of Juvenal's Sixth Satire, Ovid's *Remedia
Amoris,* and contemporary parallels such as Evelyn's *Mundus
Muliebris,* and Richard Ames's *Folly of Love,* a convention
I have dealt with in detail in relation to Swift. A second
commonplace is the use of lapdogs in the first canto. We have
long acknowledged Pope's subtle sexual references in the
poem which simultaneously lighten and strengthen the moral
implications of the Baron's act and Belinda's response. The
editor of "Rape of the Lock," Geoffrey Tillotson, observes
that lapdogs such as Shock are often equated with husbands,
or are made more significant to coquettes than their lovers, as
in Juvenal, *Tatler* Nos. 40, 47, and 121, and Farquhar's *Sir
Harry Wildair.*[7] I have already cited the lines in Robert
Gould's *Love Given O're* which suggest that lapdogs may
parallel more artificial means to satisfy women's lust. The
lines anticipate the inverted equation of man and animal,
nature and artifice, in Belinda's society: "Not louder Shrieks
to pitying Heav'n are cast, / When Husbands or when Lapdogs breathe their last" (iii.157-58). The lapdog assumes the
role of a surrogate husband, and the satire mocks such
unnatural behavior. The implication in Gould's satire is that
women will resort to any means to quench their insatiable
desire. For Belinda, the suggestion is only of her innocent
tendency toward disproportion. Swift also employs the idea
of lapdogs being artificial and ineffectual substitutes for love
or sexual satisfaction. Men of wit write "Poems address'd to
great Men's Whores; or other Lap-Dog Cures for Sores"

("Panegyric on Dr. Swift," l. 36)—the sores of a prostitute's pox cannot be cured by the lick of a lapdog.

In Richard Ames's *Folly of Love* women's sexuality can be temporarily assuaged by a lapdog: "Lap-dogs and D——s serve as much to cure / Their am'rous customary Calenture, / As men in Fevers, when they drink small Beer, / Which makes the Fit return but more severe." Perhaps the well-known and seemingly innocent lines in which Belinda rouses herself from a blissful dreaming vision of a lover allude to something more explicitly sexual: "when *Shock,* who thought she slept too long / Leapt up, and wak'd his Mistress with his Tongue" (i.115-16).[8]

Another issue in "Rape of the Lock," significant in determining how and in what way Pope is critical of Belinda, is the question of whether she seeks a husband or merely power over men. Cleanth Brooks suggests that Pope's humanism leads him to regard "virginity as essentially a negative virtue, and its possession, a temporary state." Belinda flies from spinsterhood, "the worst of all possible ills."[9] Similarly Ralph Cohen argues that Belinda should have accepted losing her virginity as naturally and gracefully as the sun rises and sets.[10] But Hugo Reichard, placing the "Rape" in the context of the *Tatler* and *Spectator,* maintains there is "not the slightest sign that she is meditating matrimony."[11]

Pope finds Belinda much flawed, but I find no convincing evidence that her failure includes a fleeing from marriage. The state of spinsterhood is never the butt of his attacks, and his models for such satires were plentiful. In *Satyr Upon Old Maids,* unmarried women are accused of being rebels against human nature, wicked vermin feeding on the earth and bringing forth no fruit. In fact, a frequent theme in Pope's other poetry is the tyranny of custom, particularly the custom of marriage. Women have "no guard but virtue, no redress but tears," he writes in "To Belinda on the Rape of the Lock." In the "Epilogue to *Jane Shore,*" he makes Mrs. Old-field comment, "And did not wicked custom so contrive, / We'd be the best, good-natur'd things alive." Most pertinent of all is the "Epistle to Miss Blount, with the Works of Voiture":

Too much *your Sex* is by their Forms confin'd,
Severe to all, but most to Womankind;
Custom, grown blind with Age, must be your Guide
Your Pleasure is a Vice, but not your Pride;
By nature yielding, stubborn but for Fame;
Made Slaves by Honour, and made Fools by Shame.
Marriage may all those petty Tyrants chace,
But sets up One, a greater, in their Place;
Well might you wish for Change, by those accurst,
But the last Tyrant ever proves the worst.
Still in Constraint your suff'ring Sex remains,
Or bound in formal, or in real Chains;
While Years neglected for some Months ador'd,
The fawning Servant turns a haughty Lord.[12] [ll. 31-44]

As in "Epistle to a Lady," each bit of praise for Belinda in
"Rape of the Lock" is mitigated by satiric diminution. Her
lively looks and sprightly mind are "unfix'd" (ii.10). The
power of her beauty also inspires the destruction of mankind.
She wins at cards but thirsts for fame. Cleanth Brooks's
comments on Pope's ambiguous response to Belinda still
seem valid. Pope projects "amused patronage," but not contempt: "For, in spite of Pope's amusement at the irrationality of that mind, Pope acknowledges its beauty and its
power."[13]

The reader does relinquish more and more sympathy for
Belinda as the poem progresses. In the first three cantos
Belinda's affectation, self-worship, and desire for fame are
gently mocked, but the responsibility for instilling such ideas
in her head rests with the sylphs, the spirits of deceased
women. Women may seem giddy, but the rhythm and pattern
of the sylphs guide their hearts and minds. In this context of
levity, Ariel's warning to beware mankind hardly seems serious. We continue to feel admiration, though somewhat
constrained, for the power of Belinda's sparkling beauty.
Even at the moment of the rape, Clarissa's seeming betrayal
in assisting the Baron musters support for Belinda as victim.
Her excessive reaction to the act of cutting, however, again
diminishes our sympathy, and, more emphatically, it links

her to the spirits of her dead sisters and to the spleen which rules "the Sex to Fifty from Fifteen, / Parents of Vapors and of Female Wit, / Who give th'*Hysteric* or *Poetic* Fit" (iv.58-60). Belinda ignores the perfectly sensible advice of Clarissa to yield to custom and necessity, and to rise above her sisters by displaying equanimity and maturity rather than the mere *appearance* of "graceful Ease, and Sweetness void of Pride" she had earlier put on at her dressing table. Apparently Pope urges us to forgive Clarissa's bringing about the rape so that she can unfold the moral, to forgive her because she offers Belinda the opportunity to develop true honor. The only way Belinda can survive our contempt for her hysteria is through the grace of the poet, who seems to succeed—by appealing to her vanity—where Clarissa had failed. The poet, unlike Clarissa, does not demand that she shift morals, only that she cease to demand restoration of the lock:

> Then cease, bright Nymph! to mourn thy ravish'd Hair
> Which adds new Glory to the shining Sphere!
> Not all the Tresses that fair Head can boast
> Shall draw such Envy as the Lock you lost.
> For, after all the Murders of your Eye,
> When, after Millions slain, your self shall die;
> When those fair Suns shall sett, as sett they must,
> And all those Tresses shall be laid in Dust;
> *This Lock*, the Muse shall consecrate to Fame,
> And mid'st the Stars inscribe Belinda's Name! [v.141-50]

Pope's attitude toward Belinda mocks while it admires, but he also airs grievances toward the sex. For Belinda displays the worst characteristics of frivolous women, and the appeal which concludes her violent response is to her basest impulses—her lust for power and fame—though of course as Pope's creation she provides those very achievements to her creator.

Pope's attitude toward women in "To a Lady" (1734/35), the second of four *Epistles to Several Persons* (later called *Moral Essays*) presents similar problems of ambiguity. Pope shows his awareness of the long tradition of antifeminist satires in the poem, and the poem relies on the reader's knowledge of popular antifeminist commonplaces. In "To a Lady" one virtuous lady contrasts to a medley of perverse and scandalous women, and the poem echoes La Bruyère's judgment a half century earlier: *"Les femmes sont extrêmes; elles sont meilleures ou pire que les hommes."*[14] The less principled women (especially Rufa, Atossa, Philomedé, Cloe, and even Queen Caroline) have attracted considerable critical attention, perhaps because the powerfully wicked portraits are enticingly topical. The single ideal character who combines learning and virtue, however, Pope's lifetime friend Miss Martha Blount, has not been as carefully studied, in part because Miss Blount's identity poses no puzzle and because her calm dignity pales beside an Atossa's frenzy or a Cloe's heartlessness. But the meaning of "Epistle to a Lady" expands when we place Martha Blount, the ideal woman, in the context of the poem, and the poem in the context of eighteenth-century attitudes toward women.

A general structural pattern of "Epistle to a Lady" emerges in spite of its complicated textual history.[15] The poet first describes disreputable ladies with increasing detail and deepening moral seriousness in the opening two hundred lines. The portraits advance from fictitious characters to allusions to real personages, from low social rank to duchesses and queens, as their offenses become increasingly threatening to moral order.[16] We glimpse Arcadia and Pastora in passing, broadly view Rufa and Sappho, and dwell even more deeply on Atossa, who is described "From loveless youth to unrespected age" (l. 125). Disparity between art and nature widens, and we realize that the worst women seduce with the charm of sin. Then, in the second section of the poem, Pope contrasts the two sexes more generally and emphasizes woman's unceasing pursuit of pleasure and power. Woman's decline in beauty, reminiscent of Swift's "Furniture of a Woman's Mind" (1727), parallels her increasing knowledge of artful deception. The poem turns abruptly to conclude with high tribute to the lady who overcomes the sex's natural failings. The poem defies any more rigid structural classification, and Patricia Meyer Spacks has persuasively suggested that the coherence of "To a Lady" relies instead on a revelatory "movement toward understanding which can absorb all incoherences into their meanings."[17]

No single theme unifies the poem, but a number of notes are struck repeatedly; to limit the poem to one of these misses the scope and complexity of the meaning. The poem progresses in its loose structure of successive portraits by sounding a theme, playing it with variation, enhancing and multiplying the meanings, and then turning them to positive advantage in the final compliment to Martha Blount. The themes in the poem depend heavily on the antifeminist context for their meaning, and before examining "To a Lady" in greater detail, I will discuss elements of eighteenth-century womanhood relevant to the poem. I am not, of course, implying that Pope necessarily made reference to the texts in question, but rather that Pope molds an imaginative antifeminist fiction which had considerable precedent and which reappears even later in the century.

In Restoration and eighteenth-century conduct books, moral essays, sermons, biographies, and poems directed at a predominantly female audience, woman is set apart from man, "contradistinguished from the other Sex," as the argument to "Epistle to a Lady" proclaims. Each of Martha Blount's virtues is commonly embodied in eighteenth-century expectations of women—constant good humor and good sense, strong social love, and quiet unassuming wit. The assumptions concerning the nature of the ideal woman continue throughout the eighteenth century. The portrait of Mrs. Crewe which introduces Sheridan's *School for Scandal* (1777) praises the qualities Pope saw in Miss Blount. Her modesty and reserve allow her to veil her beauty and learning:

> Whate'er she says—tho' Sense appear throughout—
> Bears the unartful Hue of female Doubt.
> Deck'd with that Charm how lovely Wit appears,
> How graceful *Science* when that Robe she wears!
> Such too her Talents, and her Bent of Mind
> As speak a sprightly Heart—by Thought refin'd:

A Taste for Mirth—by Contemplation school'd;
A Turn for Ridicule, by Candour rul'd;
A Scorn of Folly—which she tries to hide;
An awe of Talent—which she owns with Pride![18] [ll. 97-106]

Yet the eighteenth-century context portrays the sex as possessing characteristics at the opposite extreme from an ideal specimen of the sex—inconstancy, fickleness, excessive self-love, and ostentatious displays of wit. Most women, according to popular tradition, are more sensitive to the spleen, more delicate, and more fragile than men. Women provoke fear because their tenuous natures may more easily dissolve into thorough moral decay. Inconstant, self-centered, and affectedly witty, the female sex often attempts to outshine men when it should only reflect the light of the superior sex.

Belinda in "Rape of the Lock" dazzles men with her brilliant beauty, but women have more traditionally been symbolized by the moon which, like the goddess Cynthia, may represent the contrary qualities of inconstancy and frigidity. In an essay defending women against such uncharitable charges, "Sophia" notes that men consistently argue that "the greatest part of our sex have but short, lucid intervals;— but sudden flashes of reason which vanish in a minute;—we have a resemblance of that planet, which is dark of itself, and only shines by borrow'd light;—our wit has but a false lustre, more fit to surprise by admiration than deserve it;—we are enemies to reflection;—the majority of us only reason at hazard, think by sallies, and discourse by rote."[19] Of course, men who succumb to passion endanger order and encourage disproportion, but it is a commonplace of eighteenth-century treatises that women possess greater inconstancy and less capacity for reason than the other sex. A "softer man," woman deceives man with her brittle capricious mind. Lady Mary Chudleigh (1656-1710), among others, finds this particular propensity dismaying:

I know most People have false Idea's of Things; they think too superficially to think truly; they find it painful to carry on a Train of Thoughts; with this my own

Sex are principally chargeable; We are apt to be misled by Appearances, to be govern'd by Fancy, and the impetuous Sallies of a sprightly Imagination, and we find it too laborious to fix them; we are too easily impos'd on, too credulous, too ready to hearken to every soothing Flatterer, every Pretender to Sincerity, and to call such Friends as have not the least Title to that sacred Name.[20]

The female sex's susceptibility to flattery springs from its inherent excessive self-absorption. Thomas Brown's *Legacy for the Ladies,* a catalogue of women in extremes, specifically contends that women's self-love presents a real danger: "When once a Woman is so far infatuated with Self-Love, as to shake Hands with her Modesty, she becomes the most dangerous and ungovernable Monster that is; her Pride puts every Action, every Word, nay every Incident and Circumstance, how Minute so ever, into false Lights: Every uncommon Civility she looks upon as Adoration, and the most notorious Flattery for Truth." Brown remarks on the tenacity of self-love, and that from "the Desires which *Self-Love* inspires us with, are produced all those various Niceties *incident* to *Women,* viz. *Pre-possession, Carelessness,* Vanity, Indulgence, Idleness, and an Hundred other Defects, which they pass under the Notion of the natural *Dualities* of their Sex."[21] Self-love is particularly deplorable in eighteenth-century women because it may encourage male profligacy and disrupt expectations between the sexes. Addison's *Spectator* No. 128 (Friday, 27 July 1711) argues that women encourage foolish men: "To be short, the Passion of an ordinary Woman for a Man, is nothing else but Self-love diverted upon another Object: She would have the Lover a Woman in every thing but the Sex."[22] And Flavia, William Law's negative model in *A Serious Call to a Devout and Holy Life,* endangers her soul with her extraordinary attention to herself: "Flavia would be a *miracle* of *Piety,* if she was but half so careful of her soul, as she is of her body. The rising of a *pimple* in her face, the sting of a *gnat,* will make her keep her room two or three days, and she thinks they are very *rash* people, that don't take care of things in time. This makes her so over-careful of her *health,* that she never thinks she is well enough."[23]

The imagined activities of the undesirables in the portrait gallery of "To a Lady" contradict every expectation of appropriate and decorous behavior in the sex. The narrator particularly accuses each lady in turn of flaunting the very aspects of her person that ought not be revealed. Self-love is reprehensible, and to display it openly is worse. If women insist on cultivating wit, they are best advised to hide their learning and talents from the superior male sex, according to the tradition that associates wit with whoring. Eighteenth-century antifeminist narratives often complain that women seek knowledge as a form of self-love. The author of *The Art of Knowing Women* (1730) writes in disgust that he left the library of Clorinda, a learned lady, "fully convinced that *Learning* in *Women* is nothing but an extravagant *Self-Conceit,* upheld by a *lively Imagination,* which dazzles *shallow Wits* who look no farther than the bare *Surface of Things.*"[24] The wit of women, when carried to extremes, makes them violent, quarrelsome, and potentially destructive of social order. Women's immorality is most often associated with their vanity about learning. Thomas Brown accuses women of easily yielding their virginity when lovers flatter the quality of their minds: "Wit in *Women,* is like *Metal* in a Blind *Horse*; it serves only to hazard their Shins. The *Vanity* of shewing it, exposes 'em to all *Company*; and it often happens, that in a numerous *Acquaintance,* where they strive to establish an *Empire,* they make *Shipwreck* of their *Reputation,* and sometimes of their Vertue."[25]

Even Bluestocking Elizabeth Montagu, representative of the attitude toward wit prevailing later in the century, suspects learned women of loose morals. After reading Laetitia Pilkington's *Memoirs,* Mrs. Montagu remarks on her unfortunate misalliance of woman's wit and immorality: "It is often said that Wit is a dangerous quality; it is there meant that it is an offensive weapon, and is a perilous thing in society; but Wit in women is apt to have other bad consequences; like a sword without a scabbard it wounds the wearer and provokes assailants. I am sorry to say the generality of women who have excelled in wit have failed in chastity."[26] Similarly, Mrs. Sarah Chapone complains in a 1750 letter to George Ballard, author of *Memoirs of Eminent Ladies* (1752), that "Female authors, seem at present, to be debauching the taste and manners of the world."[27] The boldness of witty women is especially pronounced at mid-century, when diarists such as Pilkington, Charlotte Charke, and Teresa Constantia Phillips, unlike their more circumspect predecessors, publish detailed accounts of the scandalous behavior. *The Heroines: or, Modern Memoirs* (1751), a poem by Richard Graves in the antifeminist tradition, bemoans women's forsaking chastity, and its corollary, taking up the pen:

> Not so of Modern Wh-res th'illustrious train,
> Renown'd Constantia, Pilkinton, & Vane—
> Grown old in Sin, and dead to amorous Joy,
> No Acts of Penance *their* great Souls employ—
> Without a Blush, behold, each Nymph advance
> The Conscious Heroine of her own Romance:
> Each Harlot triumphs in her Loss of Fame,
> And boldly prints—& publishes her Shame.[28]

The potential threat of brash female wits and writers is sometimes treated with gentler humor. In *The Female Mentor,* a series of conversations "edited" by Honoraria from conversations of the female mentor, Amanda, comes a letter from a complaining husband. "My wife," he writes, "instead of attending to domestic concerns, and taking proper care of her children, is surrounded by wits and pedants; she is a poetess, and passes almost her whole time in composing, transcribing, and correcting. In the mean time her family is neglected."[29] The denigration of witty women often arises, however, from the serious moral concern that women's attention can only be diverted from more appropriate domestic interests. "That men are frighted by Female pedantry, is very certain," writes James Fordyce in *Sermons to Young Women* (1766). "A Woman that affects to dispute, to decide, to dictate on every subject; that watches or makes opportunities of throwing out scraps of literature, or shreds of philosophy in every company; ... that betrays, in short, a boundless intemperance of tongue, together with an inextinguishable passion for shining by the splendor of her supposed talent; such a woman is truly insufferable." In both cases a woman who seeks knowledge will also seek control and power, the "sway" of Pope's "To a Lady." Fordyce, like *The Female Mentor*'s complaining husband, encourages women to limit themselves to the family domain: "It is not the argumentative but the sentimental talents, which give you that insight and those openings into the human heart, that lead to your principal ends as Women."[30]

The meaning of the inconstancy, self-love, and false wit of the ladies of the portrait gallery in "Epistle to a Lady" paradoxically depend on the context of these assumptions about eighteenth-century women and on our simultaneous awareness of the presence of the ideal woman as a standard in the poem. Martha Blount, the inspiration for the ideal woman, inadvertently provides the rhetorical occasion for the poem and for rehearsing the ladies' flaws: "Nothing so true as what you once let fall, / 'Most Women have no Characters at all'" (ll. 1-2). As the lady accompanies him on the tour, the poet intimately confides in her. "How many pictures of one Nymph *we* view" (l. 5), he exclaims, and he seems to respond to her gestures and to encourage her condemnation of the particular portraits. Occasionally the man and woman seem to converse (ll. 33-34, 157-60, 199-202). When the lady intermittently speaks and is spoken to throughout the poem, her sober superiority increasingly distinguishes her from the entire catalogue of unattractive, unreasonable, and immoral women who exhibit all the characteristics eighteenth-century women were cautioned against. For example, in the "Epistle" Pope compares the false glitter of inconstant women who shine with brilliant light—light which dazzles, blinds, or even destroys—to the sun. Cynthia's smile, Rufa's sparkling eyes, Sappho's diamonds, and the shining insects rising from the muck all convey the affected coquette's world early in the poem. All eyes see Silia's shimmering pimple; Calypso's eyes bewitch. Atossa "shines" in exposing knaves and fools, but in doing so reveals her own stupidity. Papillia, whose name means "butterfly," ought to shun the "amorous spark" to whom she is wedded, for a spark implies both the danger of the light of a fire and an affected fop. These affected women, like Belinda with her sparkling cross in "Rape of the Lock," attempt to rival the sun and defiantly ignore their appropriate cosmic place. The light images show the ephemeral nature of their flickering light, as well as the affected falseness of fanciful women. In a passage which directly influenced Pope's "To a Lady," Edward Young in his own long catalogue of disagreeable women in *Love of Fame,* Satires V and VI, advises women to scorn shining fame: "Your sex's glory 'tis, to shine unknown; / Of all applause be fondest of your own."[31] Pope similarly consigns woman to a place of lesser light: "Our bolder Talents in full light display'd / Your Virtues open fairest in the shade" (ll. 201-02).

All the women in the portraits display inconstancy, since each is, like Arcadia's countess and Atossa, "by turns all Womankind!" (l. 116). Pope ironically suggests that women's changes are part of their illusory charm, but their inflammable minds may as easily ignite into fires of moral danger.[32] Women arouse men's passions when they touch the strange edges of experience that all men claim to hate, including folly, madness, and death—Calypso was "ne'er so sure our passion to create / As when she touch'd the brink of all we hate" (ll. 51-52). Like their sister Belinda, governed by fancy and imagination, the women allow inconsequential occurrences to disconcert them. Narcissa scorns good-nature; Flavia exhibits excessive spirit and quickness; Atossa epitomizes furious and violent passion; and even apathetic Cloe is incapable of generosity and love.

Significantly, the women of the portraits excite distorted and tentative human relationships, in contrast to Martha Blount. They harbor hatred and create an atmosphere that transforms them into the very objects of their scorn. Silia's kindness abruptly turns to raving; Philomedé is chaste to her husband but "frank to all beside" (l. 71); and Atossa "with

herself, or others, from her birth / Finds all her life one warfare upon earth" (ll. 117-18). "From loveless youth to
unrespected age" her social relationships are violently self-
centered, and self-love turned inward disproportionately in-
flates self-importance to mock-heroic proportions. The
women trap themselves in solipsism, and their evil envelops
the larger society as each seeks greater power and pleasure.
Even the apparently decent women—Cloe, who "when she
sees her Friend in deep despair, / Observes how much a
Chintz exceeds Mohair" (ll. 169-70), or Atossa, "Sick of herself thro' very selfishness!" (l. 146)—are potentially more
destructive to a stable society because they may deceptively
appear to be conciliators.

One measure of the immorality of the fearsome ladies of
the portraits is their commitment to false wit. Arcadia's
countess in her affected seriousness shows extravagant
foolishness. Rufa, reading Locke, is a study in disproportion
which recalls Steele's *Spectator* (No. 242) in which "Abra-
ham Thrifty," complaining that his learned nieces argue snow
is black and fire is not hot, pleads for regulation of female
literature and definition of "the difference between a Gentleman that should make Cheesecakes, and raise Paste, and a
Lady that reads *Lock,* and understands the Mathematicks."[33]
Narcissa, "now deep in Taylor and the Book of Martyrs, /
Now drinking citron with his Grace and Chartres" (ll. 63-64),
derives in part from Steele's *Ladies' Library* (1714), where on
the same shelf we find Mary de la Rivière Manley's scandalous *New Atalantis* next to Steele's *Christian Hero,* and La
Ferte's *A Discourse or Explications of the Grounds of
Dancing* next to Taylor's *The Rule and Exercises of Holy
Living.*[34] Even Narcissa's attempt to pursue religious study is
morally suspect, since she violently alternates between religion and atheism.

Calypso's dangerous cunning produces uneasiness since her
bewitching tongue proves her "less Wit than Mimic, more a
Wit than wise" (l. 48). Philomedé, seated as "Sin in state,"
openly flaunts her wit. Her head, like her womb, issues immoral fecundity and moral emptiness, both indicative of her
inability to fulfill woman's role:

Chaste to her Husband, frank to all beside,
A teeming Mistress, but a barren Bride.
What then? let Blood and Body bear the fault,
Her Head's untouch'd, that noble Seat of Thought:
Such this day's doctrine—in another fit
She sins with Poets thro' pure Love of Wit. [ll. 71-76]

She quickly falls from her pinnacle and punctures her learned public persona when she "stoops at once, / And makes her hearty meal upon a Dunce" (ll. 85-86). Philomedé pontificates while Flavia rages and whirls into impotence caused by "A Spark too fickle, or a Spouse too kind" (l. 94). A wit whose "sense" prevents her praying, Flavia exhibits virtue which, in its excess, turns to vice:

Wise Wretch! With Pleasures too refin'd to please,
With too much Spirit to be e'er at ease,
With too much Quickness ever to be taught,
With too much Thinking to have common Thought:
Who purchase Pain with all that Joy can give,
And die of nothing but a Rage to live. [ll. 95-100]

In the five short portraits which follow and which describe the stupid and silly women, Pope turns from wit to witlessness. All the themes of woman's extravagant nature echo and reecho—all of which culminate, not in a neat key to understanding the sex, but in affirming the riddle of femininity: "Woman and Fool are two hard things to hit, / For true No-meaning puzzles more than Wit" (ll. 113-14). Following these short characterizations of foolish women and almost equaling the length of Martha Blount's portrait is Atossa, "the wisest fool much Time has ever made" (l. 124). In addition to false wit, the sixty-year-old Atossa exudes furious yet powerless arrogance, affectation, misdirected piety. Again immorality is equated with wit, but on an even grander scale: "No thought advances, but her Eddy Brain / Whisks it about, and down it goes again" (ll. 121-22).[35] The whole sex is an enemy to the qualities required for serious thinking, for Atossa and her ilk scorn patience, discipline, and reason.

Because of Atossa and the rest of the foolish sex, Pope associates woman's wit with scandal.

Martha Blount's capacity "to raise the Thought" turns wit to advantage, however, and the poem is Pope's testimony to her ability to inspire true wit, unlike the rest of her sex. Martha Blount's lengthy portrait establishes her as an ideal for her sex, a norm against which we measure the highly entertaining but woefully deficient women. Her qualities are those which were praised universally, and it is not surprising that Swift extolls the same qualities in Stella. As Ronald Paulson has noted, in the birthday poems Stella, like Martha Blount, is physically mutable but permanently virtuous.[36] As the ideal woman venerated in the concluding portrait, Martha Blount functions in a multiple role within the context of the poem. After initiating the poem with her comment critical of the sex, she invites the narrator's extended diatribe. Throughout the poem she serves as a representative of the female audience which is to be convinced of the unmitigated immorality of the sex, and she is ultimately engaged on the side of the male speaker. Further, her portrait, "in exception to all gen'ral rules" (l. 275), turns the negative implications of recurring themes—especially inconstancy, self-love, and wit—into a positive and unparalleled model. Martha Blount is not the middle way but the unusual woman who has rid herself of the ruling passions, power and pleasure, which plague the whole sex. Having defied women's natural inconsistencies and contrarieties, she emerges *Semper Eadem.*[37]

The concluding portrait supports Miss Blount's self-abnegation, praises her sense and good humor, and offers enduring fame to her as a reward for virtue. Yet even in praise there is a kind of tenuousness, a suggestion that only one thin layer beneath, the ideal woman may resemble the rest of her sex. The compliment which recalls the frequent references to the blazing light of the ill-humored women begins with high tribute to Miss Blount:

Ah Friend! to dazzle let the Vain design,
To raise the Thought and touch the Heart, be thine!

> That Charm shall grow, while what fatigues the Ring
> Flaunts and goes down, an unregarded thing.
> So when the Sun's broad beam has tir'd the sight,
> All mild ascends the Moon's more sober light,
> Serene in Virgin Modesty she shines,
> And unobserv'd the glaring Orb declines. [ll. 249-56]

The lines contrast the lady's generosity, charm, and modesty with her counterparts' vanity and pursuit of pleasure. The words recall the earlier portraits and anticipate the poet's caution, "And yet, believe me, good as well as ill, / Woman's at best a Contradiction still" (ll. 269-70). The exceptional lady glows with the moon's more sober light rather than with the sun's wider, stronger sunbeam. Unlike the "Cynthia of this minute," she shines "Serene in Virgin Modesty."[38]

Similarly Pope suggests that the strained and artificial human relationships of the satiric portraits are dangerously short-lived in contrast to Martha Blount's steady fostering of social bonds. She converts the power so perverted by the rest of the sex into a positive unifying social force: "O! blest with Temper whose unclouded ray / Can make to morrow chearful as to day" (ll. 257-58). Pope had cautioned in the earlier "Epistle to Miss Blount, with the Works of Voiture" (1712) that *"Good Humour* only teaches Charms to last," and he argued that "Love, rais'd on Beauty, will like That decay" (l. 63).[39] Martha Blount, however, displays good humor and good sense with remarkable consistency. In a passage reminiscent of "Rape of the Lock," her equanimity prevails; she displays the good humor Clarissa unsuccessfully urges on Belinda: "[She] Lets Fops or Fortune fly which way they will; / Disdains all loss of Tickets, or Codille; / Spleen, Vapours, or Small-pox, above them all, / And Mistress of herself, tho' China fall" (ll. 265-68).

Woman, distinct from man and in inevitable conflict with him, wields her power for the forces of disorder and even chaos; a woman who uses her inherent contradictions to advantage may counter these forces to produce harmony:

Heav'n, when it strives to polish all it can
Its last best work, but forms a softer Man;
Picks from each sex, to make its Fav'rite blest,
Your love of Pleasure, our desire of Rest,
Blends, in exception to all gen'ral rules,
Your Taste of Follies, with our Scorn of Fools,
Reserve with Frankness, Art with Truth ally'd.
Courage with Softness, Modesty with Pride,
Fix'd Principles, with Fancy ever new;
Shakes all together, and produces—You. [ll. 271-80]

In this final series of paradoxes, the woman to whom the
poem is addressed resembles the Queen in that we are only allowed to know her general qualities—to know her exterior
rather than her hidden core. If we could see beneath the
Queen's garment we might find the artificial pieces of Swift's
"beautiful young nymph" or a pregnant lady or a putrid pox.
The Queen's portrait is "varnished out," a coat of varnish
subtly conveying the need to preserve the Queen from human
decay: "That Robe of Quality so struts and swells, / None see
what Parts of Nature it conceals" (ll. 189-90). The Queen is
inscrutable because she is the Queen; the venerable lady is
inscrutable because the poet idealizes her. We see that her
portrait is not firmly grounded in plain diction, and a kind of
specificity which might hint at her cracks and wrinkles is
lacking. Only the entourage of ladies preceding her is
described with particular references to spleen, vapors, and
smallpox. Pope delicately balances the way in which Martha
Blount is both the subject of panegyric and precariously like
the sisters whom we all find morally repugnant. The unex-
ampled portrait of Martha Blount does not ease or negate the
moral earnestness of the earlier portraits; it intensifies the disdain the narrator affects toward the sex.
    Since Martha Blount shares women's inconsistencies, the
satire may be understood to idealize her only by exonerating
her from most characteristics of her sex. She is heaven's "last
best work," "a softer Man," and an "exception to all gen'ral
rules." She is a phoenix who rises from the ashes of her fallen
sex. Within the tradition, the idealized woman, more angelic

than human, is in more than one account thought to be rarer than a phoenix. An anonymous gentleman, refuting Sophia's pamphlet *Woman Not Inferior to Man* (1739), argues that beauty, softness, delicacy, and grace are rare. "But such a one," he wrote, "is too delicate a Work for Nature to produce in every Century; 'Tis like a Phoenix, the Prodigy of an Age; and such a Miracle of Completeness but serves to make the rest of the Sex more contemptible by Comparison as Michael painted with the rebel Angels shews the Fiends more frightful."[40] Pope himself, in a gracious response to a virtuous lady displeased by the poem's sweeping condemnation of the sex, answered, "Madam, I must intreat of you to observe, that I only say: 'But every WOMAN is at Heart a Rake.' This no Way affects your Ladyship, who was an Angel, when you were young, and now advancing into Life, are almost already become a Saint."[41]

The force of the generalizing section on the "whole sex of Queens" which follows the denunciation of specific women also holds Martha Blount aloof from the rest of her sex. Though "*Most* Women have no Characters at all," "ev'ry Woman is at heart a Rake" and "ev'ry Lady would be Queen for life." As Owen Ruffhead remarked in explicating the poem, "We see the perpetual necessity that women lie under of disguising their ruling passion, which is not the case in men. Now the variety of arts employed to this purpose must needs draw them into infinite contradictions."[42] Thus the reader of "To a Lady" is led along with Martha Blount to agree that the rest of the sex is contemptible, and, in spite of the disclaimer in the advertisement, she *is* entertained at the expense of her sex. The moral force of the poem arises as much from Martha Blount's presence as from the portraits of undesirables. The estimable lady becomes, as Patricia Meyer Spacks argues, a metaphor "for the whole range of positive being and action open to women,"[43] but just as significantly her portrait becomes a complex metaphor for the uncertainty of most women's ability to inspire and sustain universal harmony. "The Epistle to a Lady" acknowledges with a rare psychological acumen the way in which we are often most attracted to that we most despise or fear.

While the dominant object of satire in Pope's and Swift's poetry includes inconstant women without character who worship at the twin altars of pleasure and power, and trivial women who waste their lives, the counterpart poetic fictions are the idealized Stella, who combines "manly Soul" with "Female Clay," and Martha Blount, "a softer man." Both Pope and Swift commend the women for inspiring friendship and love, but especially in the case of Pope, Martha Blount does not pulsate with sensuality. While Stella is modest, Pope's ideal woman is virginal.[44] Martha Blount lacks the wrinkles that endear Stella to Swift and to the reader. Stella somehow escapes this etherealization. Though not sensual, her sneezes and bleary eyes make her poetic fiction retain its body. In the idealized portrait of Martha Blount, she retains her womanhood—but just barely, for "to unsex" a lady means to divest her of the typical qualities of her sex, as well as to deprive her of her sexuality. The ideal woman's very ethereality, her chastity, and her ability to embody moral and social mores transform her from the fortyish old maid whom Pope admired to a symbol of domestic order who inspires the family the poet Pope grants her—husband, daughter, and sister. And of course angels have no sex.

Pope subtly exploits the antifeminist tradition and employs most of its assumptions, and in addition he combines that tradition with the impulse toward panegyric. When antifeminist satire begins to blend with romance, however, it brings about its own demise for a time. Pope avoids such an artistic dilemma by keeping both the desirable and the undesirable qualities of the sex alive and magnetically attractive. Women are still the object of satire because of characteristics inherent in their sex. At the same time he encourages our understanding of women's situation and uses the satiric mode to capture the contradictory impulses women inspire. Within the asexual ideal, he keeps them forever in unresolved conflict.

IX

Conclusion

The personal views of the satirists we have considered here are elusive, but what is as intriguing as the extent of their personal misogyny is the way their rhetorical stance sets up an imaginative satiric fiction that draws on the antifeminist tradition to serve diverse ends. The most interesting exploitations of the tradition employ its assumptions—that women are unruly monsters, that women are valued principally for beauty, that masculinized women are perverse—and turn away from the most flagrant extremes. By the mid-eighteenth century, few use antifeminist satire as a weapon to rhyme women dead; they use the notion of women in extremes—loved and hated, angel and whore, creator and destroyer—to set up a field of polarities, a fertile matrix of artistic possibilities within the satiric myth. The pamphlet wars of the Restoration manipulate the tradition to set forth the myth of a common lustful enemy in an apocalyptic vision of the sex. Butler, Rochester, Dryden, Swift, Young, Pope, and others seem to turn that antifeminist tradition to complex purposes. They defend male superiority, create an illusion of power, sustain classical and Christian myths about women, assault an object of love, urge men to abolish their romantic notions, indicate the complexity of the world women inhabit, and even attempt to reform the sex. In Swift's and Pope's works the poems are less a means to confirm traditional values than an opportunity to expose the myths by which men and women live and to reveal the sometimes ludicrous attitudes

160 The Brink of All We Hate

of both sexes. In Swift's case the satires offer no *rara avis,* but the poems on Stella postulate a counter satiric fiction that bears striking resemblance to a real woman subject to human flaws. And Pope offers in the place of ancient myths a new myth of an angelic ideal.

Perhaps the satires served a legitimate social function in urging men to restrain their lust, and a moral function in urging them to avoid promiscuity or adultery. Early satires certainly exhort men to rise above lust, to suppress their physical desires, to avoid marriage on the one hand and illegitimate children on the other. At the same time the imaginative fiction of the satire allows a peek into the mystery of the unknown. The satires repeatedly demystify the mystique of feminine ritual, the boudoir, female conversation, and sexual desire. Women writers often express their sense of entrapment in the myths men have created for them, for the satires transfer responsibility for sin, for frivolity, for inconstancy, to one sex. The male satirists seem to find the uncertainty and ambiguity of satire—its tolerance of a masked satiric voice and a multiplicity of effects—particularly suited to addressing woman, the object of both love and hate.

When satire begins to blend with romance, it allows the extremes of the antifeminist myth to subside in favor of a pallid middle—a real woman, flawed, wrinkled, but perhaps witty and wise. Satire and romance share the common bond that each attempts to neutralize the object of hate or the object of affection. To idealize a woman may allow a man to deprive her of personhood, to make her less real, less human, less capable of feeling. Theorists of satire frequently refer to the love/hate relationship between the satirist and his victim, a relationship particularly applicable here. The satirist prefers to maintain the tie between himself and his victim, between fascination and disgust, "yet this very relationship provokes his desire to inflict the remedial pain of derision or anger."[1] The eighteenth century finds a new union between lustful sex and sensibility, and simultaneously the satiric impulse to degrade women as a sex dissipates as sympathy for the loved one increases.[2]

The decline in satires after Young and Pope has been variously attributed to the sense of the burden of the tradition, the belief that generic conventions had been exhausted, the changing expectations of the audience, and the tendency of the satirist to make increasingly frequent reference to his own feelings and the feelings of his satiric victim.[3] Late eighteenth-century satires on women allow the victim to have emotions which endear her to the reader, a characteristic fatal to Juvenalian wit. Of course, fewer satires of all types were written in the mid- to late eighteenth century. Peter Hughes puts it succinctly: "In time, and in England that time came around 1750, satire destroys itself in destroying the heroic tropes and myths it needs to survive."[4] The familiar conventions of satires on women appear occasionally after 1750, but frequently the tradition is turned to a less sexist purpose. For example, John Wilkes's *An Essay on Woman* (1764) uses the tradition to satirize Warburton's edition of Pope's *Essay on Man* rather than attempting to reform the sex. Many imitations of "The Rape of the Lock" and "Epistle to a Lady" appear, but their self-conscious parody calls attention to itself rather than to the faults of the sex.

The idealized woman, so noticeably absent from seventeenth-century satire, arises in the eighteenth century within the context of satires like Pope's. Women paradoxically have been metamorphosed from embodying the disorder that men fear to embodying the values men seek.[5] But one image does not so much replace the other as coexist with it, as the myths of feminine weakness and passivity and of woman as guardian of moral values stand beside the satiric myth of the characterless woman to mock it.

In addition, this chaste and obedient woman, like an angel, is also fragile and requires patriarchal protection. The suffering pathetic maidens sentimentalize woman's supposed inferiority, and as a literary type they foster the myth of the weaker sex. At its worst, chivalry can even serve as a mask for mistreatment and degradation. When the myth of satire, "the brink of all we hate," becomes that for which society can be indicted, the sensibility shifts. Such women, paradoxically fallen from sinner to saint, become the object of pity and fear, but not the object of hate. The greater interest in the social causes for women's supposed inferiority, as demonstrated, for example, by the translation and reprinting of the Sophia pamphlets, suggests a greater tendency to believe that women are capable of reform if they are approached with reasoned arguments for that reform. Though a woman is still held accountable for marital infidelity in the mid-eighteenth century, the reasons for her loose morals or adultery are of greater interest and concern in evaluating her errors.[6] A woman understood is less a tyrant or whore or goddess than a real being, and such beings do not lend themselves as easily to vitriolic satiric treatment.

It is a delicate matter to create a female character whose temptations will not inspire others to fall and whose fallen nature will repel rather than attract followers. When John Cleland, author of *Fanny Hill*, read Laetitia Pilkington's scandalous *Memoirs* in 1749, he told the publisher that it possessed "a great deal of nature, which is enough to recommend it; but the one reflexion and a very Just and favourable one to the sex in general has occurred to me on the perusal, to wit, that this woman would have, in all probability, made an irreproachable wife, had she not been married to such a villain, as her whole history shows her husband to have been: and indeed to do that sex Justice, most of their errors are originally owing to our treatment of them: they would be [to us?] what they ought to be, if we [would be?] to them what we ought to be."[7]

The antifeminist satiric impulse is still expressed in the later eighteenth century in comic stereotypes such as Smollett's spinster Tabitha Bramble, Sheridan's Lydia Languish and Mrs. Malaprop, Sterne's "my mother," and Fanny Burney's Bluestocking, Mrs. Selwyn. But Samuel Johnson, in spite of his famous saying regarding women, preachers, and dogs, creates an intelligent woman in Rasselas's sister Nekayah, and he urges the learned astronomer to "fly to business or to Pekuah" to seek female counsel in order to conquer the excesses of the imagination. As the emphasis shifts to the newer version of the fiction, satiric attacks begin to dissolve into a chivalrous protection of women from men's violent words. For example, *The Female Congress; or the Temple of Cotytto* (1779), a mock-heroic poem in four cantos, moves from the conventional disclaimer about references to particular women to a disavowal of the Juvenalian tradition from which it derives:

> Juvenal, with the best intentions in the world, has let fall many things shocking enough to a modest ear. In condemning satire for its freedom, people are apt to forget its end, and the persons to whom it is addresst; and, at the very moment when it is reflecting the image of deformity, they are angry that the figure is indecent, or ungraceful. Satire is not intended for the innocent and spotless, but the vicious and contaminated to whom pictures of depravity are no novelty. . . . Should the chaste virgin at any time meet with expressions or images in the works of the satirist, that wound her delicacy, let her recollect, that the painting was not designed for her inspection.[8]

The ostensible purpose of *The Female Congress* is to quell "the frequent violations of her marriage bed, and the rising licentiousness of female manners," but the poem is mild, not obscene, and as anti-Methodist and anti-Scots as it is anti-feminist.

Similarly, Reverend Richard Polwhele's *The Unsex'd Females* (1798) impels men to protect women from sexual knowledge. For Polwhele, unsexed females act like men, but they are not desexualized angels. The satire, aimed at Mary Wollstonecraft, includes Hannah More as his standard norm throughout, and he integrates her into the satire. Modest, natural, beautiful, and a cheerful inspiration to all, Hannah More contrasts with strident Mary Wollstonecraft, who claims superiority to men. The satirist compares the two and says he prefers the blush of modesty to the sparkle of intelligence. Laetitia Barbauld, Mary Robinson, Charlotte Smith, Mary Hays, and other female authors supposedly encourage women to bare their necks and breasts according to the latest fashion. Worse, they encourage boys and girls to "botanize together" ("Dissent its organ of unhallow'd lust, / And fondly gaze the titillating dust"[9]) but being a female author is not, in itself, subject to satire. Montagu, Carter, Chapone, Piozzi, Burney, and others are congratulated on their learning and held up for our admiration. The satire clarifies that being a woman is not inherently a problem, but rather it is woman's attempt to be a man that threatens social order. Using one of the sex against the entire sex in the familiar anti-feminist satiric tradition, Polwhele maintains that women's spheres are distinct from men's but equal. Such distinct natures and distinct spheres are the privileges to which women are entitled.

Such poems as *Female Virtues* (1787) claim that women only need to be shown the error of their ways in order to reform; such a belief dissipates the urge to satire and creates in its stead poems in which the praise of the ideal woman equals or exceeds the blame of disreputable women. In *Female Virtues* the happiness of a modest woman, contrasted with the condition of one who has been seduced, is followed by a description of Truth and the ill effects of indolence and luxury. Such poems are stultifying fare in contrast to the lively vituperation of the antifeminist tradition. In *The Female Aegis* (1798)[10] women are urged to be satisfied with the smaller sphere of feminine influence—family, forming the manners of husbands, and molding children.

By the end of the century the mode has largely changed from verse satire to fiction and essays, and the language has changed from the obscenity of Oldham and Gould, but the assumptions concerning the appropriate spheres of female activity are still very much in question. Richard Polwhele, Mary Hays, Mary Wollstonecraft are all part of another controversy, beyond the scope of this study, which raged at the end of the eighteenth century—a controversy based on encouraging a belief that women share men's capacity for reason. During the late decades in the century, women may have been subjected to a revived moralism and repression. For example, evidence in *The Ladies Magazine* shows that renewed Evangelicalism may well have served to reinforce traditional patterns for women.[11] Women's economic opportunities were probably not much improved at the end of the eighteenth century. It is not at all clear what effect industrialization brought to women's lives. Neil McKendrick contends that women's factory earnings, though only two-thirds of a man's pay, "were regarded as a threat to male authority, a temptation to female luxury and indulgence, and an incitement to female independence."[12] Industrialization brought deplorable labor conditions in the developing mills and factories, but it also brought increased opportunity for women to contribute to the family unit's economic well-being. What does seem clear is that by the end of the century more women read, the birth rate inclined, the death rate declined, more women became professional writers, and more produced an independent income.[13]

While the early antifeminism we have traced apparently arose from a context of religious Puritan argument, women's role in the fall of man, the subjection of women to husbands, and the concern for property and inheritance, later eighteenth-century antifeminism came from an insistence on woman's inferior capacity for reason. While early feminists readily accepted the notion that women and men had distinct but equal spheres, the later eighteenth-century feminists argued that the only inherent distinction was bodily strength, and that physical prowess was no basis for limiting women's education. For Mary Wollstonecraft, arguing against Milton, Swift, Rousseau, Dr. James Fordyce, and Dr. John Gregory, antifeminism is not just calling women names. She herself says women have learned to be sentimental, indolent, and morally weak, but she offers the counterargument that such arguments ought to be expanded to men. Calling for an end to the double standard, she blames men for women's state: "all the causes of female weakness, as well as depravity . . . branch out of one grand cause—want of chastity in men."[14] She wittily encourages women to turn Pope's sarcasm—that every woman is at heart a rake—on men. In fact, in many ways Pope's "Epistle to a Lady" serves as a subtext for *A Vindication of the Rights of Woman,* and at one point Wollstonecraft seems to be arguing directly against Pope's portrait of the ideal woman:

It follows then that cunning should not be opposed to wisdom, little cares to great exertions, or insipid soft-ness, varnished over with the name of gentleness, to that fortitude which grand views alone can inspire.

I shall be told that woman would then lose many of her peculiar graces, and the opinion of a well known poet might be quoted to refute my unqualified asser-tion. For Pope has said, in the name of the whole male sex,

'Yet ne'er so sure our passion to create,
As when she touch'd the brink of all we hate.'

In what light this sally places men and women, I shall leave the judicious to determine; meanwhile I shall con-tent myself with observing, that I cannot discover why, unless they are mortal, females should always be de-graded by being subservient to love or lust.[15]

Virtue, like the lack of virtue, she claims, is not to be sexu-ally linked, and to do so is to degrade *both* sexes. Her plea to men is to free women from the chains of tyranny and degradation—and thus to find themselves in the company of a like rational being.

Mary Wollstonecraft hopes to liberate women from the oppressive stereotypes of antifeminist satire as well as the new myths of sentimentalism, the seduced maiden, the chaste matron, and the sexless angel. She foresees in these myths an equally insidious desexualization of women: "Why are girls to be told that they resemble angels; but to sink them below women?" And elsewhere Wollstonecraft draws attention to the illogic of the myth when she writes, "Women, weak wom-en, are compared with angels; yet, a superiour order of beings should be supposed to possess more intellect than man; or, in what does their superiority consist? In the same strain, to drop the sneer, they are allowed to possess more goodness of heart, piety, and benevolence."[16] Wollstonecraft recognizes in the romantic impulse a declaration of woman's inferiority, an insidious counterpart to satire. The only logical way to introduce a paragon is to make her more than her sisters, better than her sex, or to divest her of qualities inherent in the sex. The new myth of womanhood at the end of the eighteenth century urged—even required—women to transcend the female experience.

Pope's Calypso, who "touch'd the brink of all we hate," owes her charm to her defects, for her lack of virtue, beauty, and wisdom somehow awes and bewitches her admirers. The fictions of satire created in satires on women often seem to transform the potential for men's attraction to destructive elements into attacks on the female sex in the early period, and into an earnest joke by the mid-eighteenth century. The fiction of satire creates a fertile field for reframing what is most frightening into something comic—yet always on the edge of the abyss of all that is most reprehensible.

Notes

CHAPTER I

1. "A Satyr on Charles II," in *The Complete Poems of John Wilmot, Earl of Rochester*, ed. David Vieth (New Haven: Yale Univ. Press, 1968), p. 70, ll. 14-15.

2. *Memoirs of Laetitia Pilkington, 1712-50, Written by Herself*, ed. Iris Barry (New York: Dodd, Mead, 1928), pp. 53, 103. The verbal assault on Pilkington is said in good humor and introduces a jest which compliments Pilkington to her husband. Swift, Pilkington notes, "always prefaced a compliment with an affront."

3. Katharine M. Rogers, in *The Troublesome Helpmate: A History of Misogyny in Literature* (Seattle: Univ. of Washington Press, 1966), has traced the history of misogyny from Eve to the twentieth century. In general I agree with the conclusion she draws in her chapter on the Restoration and eighteenth century—that in the period "there is a gradual softening of the prevalent attitude to women, combined with an increasing tendency toward polite disparagement" (p. 187).

4. For example, Robert C. Elliott, *The Literary Persona* (Chicago: Univ. of Chicago Press, 1981); Alvin B. Kernan, *The Plot of Satire* (New Haven: Yale Univ. Press, 1965); and Maynard Mack, "The Muse of Satire," *Yale Review* 41 (1951): 80-92.

5. The question of whether neoclassical antifeminist satires, especially those of Pope and Swift, are "projections of male anxiety and ambivalence about sexuality and control" or a literary activity influenced by the linguistic ,and cultural codes available at a certain historical moment is debated by Susan Gubar in "The Female Monster in Augustan Satire," *Signs* 3 (Winter 1977): 380-94, and in a subsequent exchange with Ellen Pollak, *Signs* 3 (Spring 1978): 728-33. I suggest that antifeminist satires can be alternately and simultaneously reflections of the historical situation and of male projections, though the emphasis in this book is on the satirist's rhetorical stance and the creation of a fiction of satire, rather than on the individual neurosis of the satirist.

6. Michael Seidel, *The Satiric Inheritance: Rabelais to Sterne* (Princeton: Princeton Univ. Press, 1979), p. 12.

7. Joseph Addison and Richard Steele, *The Spectator*, ed. Donald F. Bond

(Oxford: Clarendon Press, 1965), I: 68. All subsequent citations are to this edition.

8. Ballard Ms. 43, f. 17, Bodleian Library, Oxford. On 7 March 1735/36 Elstob apologizes to George Ballard: "Yet I do not think my self proficient enough in these Arts, to become a teacher of them." I am grateful for permission to cite this manuscript.

9. John Bennett, *Strictures on Female Education Chiefly As It Relates to the Culture of the Heart* (London, 1795; rpt., Manchester: Source Book Press, 1971), p. 88.

10. George Lillo, *The London Merchant*, ed. William H. McBurney, Regents Restoration Drama Series (Lincoln: Univ. of Nebraska Press, 1965), p. 64.

CHAPTER II

1. *De l'égalité des deux sexes* was republished in 1676, 1679, 1690, and 1691. For a useful note on François Poulain de la Barre (1647-1723), with liberal citations from the essays, consult Michael A. Seidel, "Poulain De La Barre's *The Woman As Good As the Man*," *Journal of the History of Ideas* 35 (1974): 499-508.

2. Earl Miner, *The Restoration Mode from Milton to Dryden* (Princeton: Princeton Univ. Press, 1974), p. 389. See also Miner's "In Satire's Falling City," in *The Satirist's Art*, ed. H. James Jensen and Malvin R. Zirker, Jr. (Bloomington: Indiana Univ. Press, 1972), pp. 3-27.

3. Lawrence Stone, *The Crisis of the Aristocracy, 1558-1641* (Oxford: Oxford Univ. Press, 1965), pp. 637-45.

4. Gregory King, *Natural and Politicall Observation and Conclusions upon the State and Condition of England* (London, 1696). For general studies, see Roger Thompson, *Women in Stuart England and America* (London: Routledge and Kegan Paul, 1974), pp. 31-59; and Barbara Schnorrenberg and Jean E. Hunter, "The Eighteenth-Century Englishwoman," in *The Women of England from Anglo-Saxon Times to the Present: Interpretive Bibliographical Essays*, ed. Barbara Kanner (Hamden, Conn.: Shoestring Press, 1979).

5. Dorothy Gardiner, *English Girlhood at School: A Study of Education through Twelve Centuries* (London: Oxford Univ. Press, 1929), p. 235; Myra Reynolds, *The Learned Lady in England, 1650-1760* (New York: Houghton Mifflin, 1920), pp. 27-45.

6. Ed. Paula L. Barbour, Augustan Reprint Society, no. 202 (Los Angeles: William Andrews Clark Memorial Library, 1980), pp. 3-4.

7. In "Richard Steele and the Status of Women," *Studies in Philology* 26 (1929): 326, Rae Blanchard accurately labels Fénelon, along with Richard Brathwaite, Gervase Markham, Richard Allestree, and Lord Halifax, as conservatives who believe woman is inferior by nature, custom, and biblical law.

8. *An Essay in Defence of the Female Sex in which are inserted the characters of A Pedant, A Squire, A Beau, A Vertuoso, A Poetaster, A City-critick. &c. In a Letter to a Lady By a Lady* was published in 1696 (2nd ed. 1696; 3rd, 1697; 4th, 1791). Though it has generally been attributed to Mary Astell, Myra Reynolds cites the author as Mrs. Drake, wife of James Drake, while Rae Blanchard notes

that *A Farther Essay in Defence of the Female Sex* is a literal translation of Madame de Pringy's essay. The author defends women's learning and argues against the usual charges of lust. For a recent study that underscores Astell's belief in women's separate but equal domain, see Joan K. Kinnaird, "Mary Astell and the Conservative Contribution to English Feminism," *Journal of British Studies* 19 (1979): 53-75.

9. Daniel Defoe, *An Essay on Projects* (London, 1697).

10. Lawrence Stone, *The Family, Sex and Marriage in England, 1500-1800* (New York: Harper and Row, 1977), chapter 6.

11. Alice Clark, *Working Life of Women in the Seventeenth Century* (London: George Routledge, 1919).

12. See, for example, J.J. Habakkuk, "Marriage Settlements in the Eighteenth Century," *Transactions of the Royal Historical Society*, 4th ser., 32 (1950): 15-30.

13. [Margaret Fell], *Women Speaking Justified* (1667), ed. David Latt, Augustan Reprint Society, no. 196 (Los Angeles: William Andrews Clark Memorial Library, 1979).

14. 3rd ed. (London, 1634), p. 275.

15. Christopher Hill, in *The World Turned Upside Down: Radical Ideas during the English Revolution* (London: Temple Smith, 1972), pp. 247-60, discusses the position of women, especially in radical sects like the Ranters.

16. Keith Thomas, "Women and the Civil War Sects," *Past and Present* 13 (1958): 55-56.

17. Roger Thompson, *Unfit for Modest Ears: A Study of Pornographic, Obscene and Bawdy Works Written or Published in England in the Second Half of the Seventeenth Century* (Totowa, N.J.: Rowman and Littlefield, 1979).

18. Entry for 12-13 January 1668, *The Diary of Samuel Pepys, 1668-1669*, ed. Robert Latham and William Matthews (Berkeley: Univ. of California Press, 1976), 9: 21-22.

19. David Foxon, *Libertine Literature in England, 1660-1745* (New Hyde Park, N.Y.: University Books, 1965), pp. 12-15.

20. Ibid., p. 47.

21. Simone de Beauvoir, *The Second Sex*, trans. H.M. Parshley (New York: Knopf, 1953), p. 128.

22. *Poems, 1693-1696*, ed. A.B. Chambers, William Frost, and Vinton Dearing, vol. 4 of *The Works of John Dryden*, ed. H.T. Swedenberg, Jr. (Berkeley: Univ. of California Press, 1974), p. 77.

23. Peter Elkin, in *The Augustan Defence of Satire* (Oxford: Clarendon Press, 1973), pp. 73-117, provides a convenient summary of views.

24. 26 April 1711 in *The Prose Works of Jonathan Swift*, ed. Herbert Davis (Oxford: Shakespeare Head Press, 1940) 3: 141.

25. Northrop Frye, *Anatomy of Criticism: Four Essays* (Princeton: Princeton Univ. Press, 1957), pp. 223-39.

26. Louis Bredvold, "A Note in Defense of Satire," *ELH* 7 (1940): 261.

27. Robert Elliott, "The Satirist and Society," *ELH* 21 (1954): 246.

28. *The World*, no. 9, 1 March 1753.

29. *A Tale of a Tub with Other Early Works, 1696-1707,* ed. Herbert Davis, vol. 1 of *The Prose Works of Jonathan Swift* (Oxford: Shakespeare Head Press, 1939), p. 31.

30. William Gifford, *The Satires of Decimus Junius Juvenalis, translated into English verse* (London, 1802), p. xlviii.

31. Elliott, "Satirist and Society," p. 238; idem, *The Power of Satire: Magic, Ritual, Art* (Princeton: Princeton Univ. Press, 1960), esp. pp. 3-14.

32. In his recent edition of the Semonides fragment, *Females of the Species: Semonides on Women* (London: Noyes Press, 1975), p. 23, Hugh Lloyd Jones reminds us that abuse hurled between the sexes was probably part of Greek religious ritual, and that "the notion that the abuse of women was a regular literary theme, appropriate to the iambus and having conventions of its own, seems to have much in its favour."

33. Alvin Kernan, "Aggression and Satire: Art Considered as a Form of Biological Adaptation," in *Literary Theory and Structure: Essays in Honor of William K. Wimsatt,* ed. Frank Brady, John Palmer, and Martin Price (New Haven: Yale Univ. Press, 1973), pp. 120-21.

34. Ibid., p. 123.

35. Ibid., p. 126.

36. Ibid., p. 125.

37. For discussions of Eve's role in the tradition of misogyny, see Kate Millett, *Sexual Politics* (New York: Doubleday, 1968); and Andrée Kahn Blumstein, *Misogyny and Idealization in the Courtly Romance* (Bonn: Herbert Grundmann, 1977).

38. Harold F. Brooks, "A Bibliography of John Oldham," *Oxford Bibliographical Society Proceedings* 5, pt. i (1936): 5-7; David M. Vieth, "John Oldham, the Wits and *A Satyr Against Vertue,*" *Philological Quarterly* 32 (1953): 90-93.

39. Alvin Kernan, in *The Cankered Muse: Satire of the English Renaissance* (New Haven: Yale Univ. Press, 1959) provides a thorough history of English satire.

40. John Oldham, *Some New Pieces Never before Publish'd* (London, 1684).

41. The circumstances would undoubtedly shed light on the poem since Oldham often relies on external frames and epithets to clarify the meaning of his text. See, for example, David Wykes, "Aspects of Restoration Irony: John Oldham," *English Studies* 52 (1971): 223-31.

42. John Oldham, *Satyrs Upon the Jesuits and other Pieces* (London, 1682), pp. 139-48.

43. *Misogynus: Or, A Satyr Upon Women* (London, 1682), p. 2.

44. *The Great Birth of Man or, the Excellency of Man's Creation and Endowment Above the Original of Women,* 3rd ed. by M.S. (London, 1686), p. 3.

45. The satire appears in *Pecuniae obediunt Omnia* (London, 1698), p. 123.

46. The satire, printed for Andrew Green, appeared anonymously with a paste-over imprint of 1682 [Wing G 1422]. The actual date of publication was probably 1683. The original imprint reads "London / Printed for R. Bentley in Russell— / Street near the Piazza in Covent Garden, 1683." Green simply usurped the Bentley edition. A.H. Upham cites the publication date as 1680,

probably on the authority of the *DNB,* though *Love Given O're* was written in 1680 and published in 1683. The reason for the pasted-over date is obscure. If a seventeenth-century book was suppressed by authorities, publishers of subsequent editions sometimes provided false dating in order to elude authorities seeking retribution. Thus they claimed to be selling remnants of the first edition, and simultaneously deluded purchasers into thinking they owned the rare first edition. See also Foxon, *Libertine Literature,* p. viii. Perhaps the obscenity combined with the explicit attacks on London actresses made printers hesitant to accept responsibility for the first edition of the satire. Upham also notes that *Love Given O're* has often been erroneously attributed to Tom Brown (British Museum Catalogue). Since the satire was published with *Satire Against Wooing* (1703), the title page bore Gould's name. See *Satires on Women,* ed. Felicity A. Nussbaum, Augustan Reprint Society, no. 180 (Los Angeles: William Andrews Clark Memorial Library, 1976).

47. David E. Baker, Isaac Reed, and Stephen Jones, *Biographia Dramatica: Or, A Companion to the Playhouse* (1812; rpt. N.Y.: AMS Press, 1966), 1: 293; 2: 325-26; 3: 212. The sole biographical and critical study of Robert Gould remains Eugene H. Sloane's *Robert Gould, Seventeenth-Century Satirist* (Philadelphia: Univ. of Pennsylvania Press, 1940). See also Howard Weinbrot, "Robert Gould: Some Borrowings from Dryden," *English Language Notes* 3 (1965): 36-40.

48. *The Play-House, A Satyr* is reprinted in Montague Summers, *The Restoration Theatre* (London: Kegan Paul, Tranch, Trubner, 1934), App. I, pp. 297-321.

49. See Sloane, *Robert Gould,* pp. 7-47, for more detailed biographical information.

50. This dedication to *The Sketch* (1698/99) is cited in Sloane, *Robert Gould,* p. 33.

51. All quotations from *Love Given O're, The Female Advocate,* and *The Folly of Love* are from ARS Reprint, no. 180. Other satires cited, including *Sylvia's Revenge, A Scourge for Ill Wives, The Lost Maidenhead, The Restor'd Maidenhead, A Satyr Against Wooing, Female Fireships,* and *The Pleasures of Love* are in the collection of the William Andrews Clark Memorial Library.

52. Sandra M. Gilbert and Susan Gubar, in *The Madwoman in the Attic* (New Haven: Yale Univ. Press, 1979), p. 27, demonstrate that the fear of "inconstancy" in the Victorian period represented man's fear of woman's "stubborn autonomy and unknowable subjectivity, meaning the ineradicable selfishness that underlies even her angelic renunciation of self."

53. *The New Cambridge Bibliography of English Literature,* 2: 472-73, lists Sarah Egerton, née Fige, born c. 1672, as the author of *The Female Advocate* and *Poems on Several Occasions,* together with a pastoral (1703) reissued in 1706. Jeslyn Medoff's "New Light on Sarah Fyge (Field, Egerton)," *Tulsa Studies in Women's Literature* 1 (1982): 155-75, gives full biographical detail.

54. Caroline Whitbeck, "Theories of Sex Difference," in *Women and Philosophy,* ed. Carol C. Gould and Marz W. Martofsky (New York: Putnam, 1976), pp. 54-80.

55. In the advertisement to *The Poetess,* Gould assumes or affects that

Sylvia's Revenge was written by a woman who is singly guilty of more vices than the rest of her sex combined.

56. John Dunton, in *The Nightwalker,* for example, reported that London whores were as thick as boats on the Thames. See Dudley W.R. Bahlman, *The Moral Revolution of 1688* (New Haven: Yale Univ. Press, 1957).

CHAPTER III

1. *Epicoene,* I.i. See Jean E. Gagen, *The New Woman: Her Emergence in English Drama, 1600-1730* (New York: Twayne, 1954), p. 25, for this quotation and for other examples of Amazonian women in seventeenth-century drama.

2. Poulain de la Barre, *The Woman As Good As the Man,* trans. A.L. (London, 1677), pp. 145, 149-65. Princess Amelia Sophia, George II's daughter, was touted for her masculine apparel when hunting, and one of Samuel Richardson's *Familiar Letters on the Most Important Occasions in Common Life* (1741), XC, pp. 124-26, cautions against the hermaphroditic dress of a riding outfit because "In this one Instance we do not prefer our own Likeness, and the less you resemble us, the more you are sure to charm: For a *masculine Woman* is a Character as little creditable as becoming."

3. Of Amazons throughout history, Nina Auerbach, in *Communities of Women* (Cambridge: Harvard Univ. Press, 1978), p. 4, writes, "Not only do they lack womanly biology; they lack the womanly skills that transform nature into sustenance."

4. "A Dissertation on the Amazons. From the History of the Amazons, written in French by the Abbé de Guyon," *Gentleman's Magazine* 11 (April 1741): 202-08. Apparently only the first paragraph was Johnson's work.

5. Gagen, *New Woman,* chapter 11.

6. Edward Howard, *Six Days Adventure* (London, 1671).

7. Thomas Heywood, *Gunaikeion: or, Nine Bookes of Various History Concerninge Women* (London, 1624), p. 222; reprinted in 1657.

8. Thomas D'Urfey, *A Commonwealth of Women* (London, 1685), Act III.

9. Edward Howard, *The Women's Conquest* (London, 1671), Act V.

10. *Spectator,* IV: 24-26.

11. *The Idler and the Adventurer* in *The Yale Editions of the Works of Samuel Johnson,* ed. W.J. Bate, J.M. Bullitt, and L.F. Powell (New Haven: Yale Univ. Press, 1963), 2: 272.

12. Samuel Butler, *Satires and Miscellaneous Poetry and Prose,* ed. René Lamar (Cambridge: Cambridge Univ. Press, 1928), pp. 220-21.

13. Samuel Butler, *Prose Observations,* ed. Hugh De Quehen (Oxford: Clarendon Press, 1979), pp. 44, 74, 82, 165, 171, 196, 268-70.

14. Ibid., p. 174.

15. See James E. Phillips, Jr., "The Background of Spenser's Attitude toward Women Rulers," *Huntington Library Quarterly* 5 (1941): 5-32.

16. Earl Miner, *The Restoration Mode from Milton to Dryden* (Princeton: Princeton Univ. Press, 1974), p. 188. Miner stresses, however, that Butler's *posture* is feminist.

17. Samuel Butler, *Hudibras,* ed. John Wilders (Oxford: Oxford Univ. Press, 1967), I.ii.367-68, 398.

18. George Wasserman, in *"Hudibras* and Male Chauvinism," *Studies in English Literature, 1500-1900* 16 (1976): 353, confines the importance of female power in the poem to Parts II and III. It is true that "the satiric strategy of Part I attacks a rational pride by elevating animals over men" but it also elevates women over men, as in the case of Trulla. See also Wasserman's *Samuel "Hudibras" Butler* (Boston: G.K. Hall, 1976), pp. 54-102.

19. Natalie Zemon Davis, "Women on Top: Symbolic Sexual Inversion and Political Disorder in Early Modern Europe," in *The Reversible World: Symbolic Inversion in Art and Society,* ed. Barbara Babcock (Ithaca: Cornell Univ. Press, 1978), pp. 147-90. Traditionally anthropologists have defined sex reversal as clarifying and reaffirming sexual hierarchies without changing them, but Davis (p. 170) argues that the Skimmington procession is "an expression of the struggle over change, that is, over the location of power and property within the family and without."

20. Davis, "Women on Top," p. 163, appropriately cites the motif of Phyllis riding Aristotle as the comic prototype of the woman as social critic. Disorderly women reveal the truth: "This is what happens when women are given the upper hand; and yet in some sense the men deserve it."

21. Earl Miner has called it the "most sustained argument for feminism to appear in English poetry to that time." *Restoration Mode,* p. 190.

22. *Prose Observations,* p. 4.

CHAPTER IV

1. *The Rochester-Savile Letters, 1671-1680,* ed. John Harold Wilson (Columbus: Ohio State Univ. Press, 1941), Letter III, p. 33.

2. Carole Fabricant, "Rochester's World of Inperfect Enjoyment," *Journal of English and Germanic Philology* 73 (1974): 348.

3. John E. Sitter, in "Rochester's Reader and the Problem of Satiric Audience," *Papers on Language and Literature* 12 (1976): 287, has argued in another context that Rochester's language "is subversive and aggressive, and that his poems mount an assault upon the reader and his attitudes toward language."

4. Rochester, *Complete Poems,* p. 81. (See chapter 1, note 1.) All subsequent references to Rochester's poems are to this edition.

5. See, for example, Dustin Griffin, *Satires Against Man: The Poems of Rochester* (Berkeley: Univ. of California Press, 1973), pp. 124-25.

6. Griffin, in ibid., pp. 25-35, discusses "St. James's Park" in regard to pastoral and Cavalier models.

7. Miner, *Restoration Mode,* p. 375.

8. This is probably a commonplace. It also appears in the second Prologue to *Sodom: The Quintessence of Debauchery,* uncertainly attributed to Rochester; introduction by Albert Ellis (North Hollywood, Cal.: Brandon House Books, 1966), p. 56.

9. Alexander Pope, *The Rape of the Lock and Other Poems,* ed. Geoffrey

Tillotson, Twickenham Edition, 3rd ed. (New Haven: Yale Univ. Press, 1962), 2: 147, 154.

10. Dr. ——, *The Second Volume of Miscellaneous Works* (London, 1705).

11. Anne Righter, "John Wilmot, Earl of Rochester," *Proceedings of the British Academy* 53 (1967): 52.

12. See especially Richard E. Quaintance, "French Sources of the Restoration 'Imperfect Enjoyment' Poem," *Philological Quarterly* 42 (1963): 190-99.

13. Ibid., p. 191.

14. Griffin, *Satires Against Man*, p. 95.

15. Here I disagree with Griffin who argues that the "'eager desires' have been shown (in ll. 1-18) to be shared by body and mind alike; shame and rage may prevent the lover's 'recovery' but have nothing to do with the initial problem, caused as it is by an over-active body." *Satires Against Man*, p. 97.

16. It is worth noting that Rochester does not emphasize the excess of love in the way that Aphra Behn had done in "The Disappointment." See Quaintance, "French Sources," pp. 198-99.

17. Fabricant, "Rochester's World," p. 350.

18. Reba Wilcoxon, "Pornography, Obscenity, and Rochester's 'The Imperfect Enjoyment,'" *Studies in English Literature, 1500-1900* 15 (1975): 389.

19. Verse satires with similar themes include Robert Gould's *The Poetess* (1688) and its revised version *A Satyrical Epistle to the Author of Sylvia's Revenge* (1691), as well as standard *memento mori* lines, e.g., "The fairest Face that ever Nature made, / A little Sickness soon will make it fade, / 'Tis nought but Worms and Dust in Masquerade," a triplet appearing in Captain Alexander Radcliff's *A Satyr Against Love, and Women* (London, 1682).

20. For the association of the "scribbling itch" with promiscuity, see, for example, Myra Reynolds, *The Learned Lady in England, 1650-1760* (New York: Houghton Mifflin, 1920), pp. 372-419.

21. Howard Weinbrot has remarked on the perversion of God's law in the poem in "The Swelling Volume: The Apocalyptic Satire of Rochester's *Letter from Artemisia in the Town to Chloe in the Country*," *Studies in the Literary Imagination* 5 (1972): 24. "Spiritual love surrenders to secular love, God's design to woman's," he writes, and the lady's tale is a "parody of divine purpose." Nature seems to be of as much concern as the divine to Artemisia or Rochester, however.

22. John Harold Wilson, *The Court Wits of the Restoration: An Introduction* (Princeton: Princeton Univ. Press, 1948), pp. 131-32.

23. Anne Righter has suggested that Artemisia is a sympathetic character who in turn evidences understanding of the fine lady's misuse of her intelligence and Corinna's lack of self-knowledge. "John Wilmot, Earl of Rochester," pp. 47-69.

24. Griffin, *Satires Against Man*, p. 133.

CHAPTER V

1. For Dryden's translation, see *Poems 1693-1696*, pp. 145-203, ll. 5-7. (See chapter 2, note 22, above.) All subsequent references are to this edition.

2. William S. Anderson, in "Juvenal 6: A Problem in Structure," *Classical Philology* 51 (1956): 93, argues that Juvenal's central theme is *Pudicitia*. Woman "has lost her womanhood (*pudor*, 21-285); in its place, she has adopted viciousness (*saeva luxuria*, 301-643)."

3. *The Satires of Decimus Junius Juvenalis*, published in 1692, appeared in various editions in 1693, 1697, 1702, 1711, 1713, and 1735, and was reprinted in 1754.

4. William Walsh, *Dialogue Concerning Women, Being a Defence of the Sex. Written to Eugenia* (London, 1691), preface by Dryden and p. 79.

5. *Poems, 1693-1696*, p. 145.

6. See William S. Anderson, *Anger in Juvenal and Seneca*, University of California Publications in Classical Philology, 19, no. 3 (Berkeley: Univ. of California Press, 1964), pp. 127-79. Niall Rudd, in "Dryden on Horace and Juvenal," *University of Toronto Quarterly* 32 (1963): 155-69, also suggests that Juvenal's satiric technique involves overpowering the reader's rational faculties. Among those who have assumed the voice of the satirist was identical to Juvenal's is Gilbert Highet in *Juvenal the Satirist* (Oxford: Clarendon Press, 1954), p. 269 n.17, who suggests that "Juvenal had begun his life with normal instincts, and had then been so disgusted by women that he turned to active homosexuality." Anderson, however, uses persona theory to identify five satiric contradictions in Juvenal, but not peculiar to Juvenal alone. Those conflicts include: (1) the plain speaker who employs skillful rhetoric; (2) the truthteller who distorts facts; (3) the man who apparently hates vice and glories in sensational detail; (4) the moralist who indulges in sadism; and (5) the rationalist who rages with mad passion.

7. Carnochan suggests that the moral climate in the 1690s discouraged such outright obscenity, while Paul Korshin responds that he knows "of no evidence that any of them was concerned with censorship of lewd publications or, in fact, that there was substantial decline in the bawdy or abusive contents of the popular press during the decade in question." The exchange appears in *TLS*, 21 Jan. 1972, pp. 73-74, and 17 March 1972, pp. 307-08. See also D.S. Thomas, *The Library*, 5th ser., 24 (1969): 51-55.

8. Sir Robert Stapylton, Epistle Dedicatory, *The First Six Satyrs of Juvenal, with Annotations clearing the obscurer places out of the History, Lawes, and Ceremonies of the Romans* (Oxford, 1644).

9. Stapylton published all of Juvenal's satires in 1647, and a revised edition, *Mores Hominum, the Manners of Men*, in 1660. The Sixth Satire was seldom printed singly during the period. For a full publication history, see G.L. Broderson, "Seventeenth-Century Translations of Juvenal," *Phoenix: The Journal of the Classical Association of Canada* 7 (1953): 57-76. Robert Calvin Whitford, in "Juvenal in England, 1750-1802," *Philological Quarterly* 7 (1928): 9-16, discusses the continuing popularity of Juvenal in the eighteenth century. Dryden treats Holyday and Stapylton with considerable disdain in the conclusion to the *Discourse Concerning Satire*.

10. *Decimus Junius Juvenalis and A. Persius Flaccus translated and illustrated . . . by Barten Holyday* (Oxford, 1673). All subsequent references are to this text.

Holyday's version was begun before Stapylton's appeared, though it was not published until 1673.

11. Henry Fielding, "Juvenal's Sixth Satire Modernized in Burlesque Verse," *Miscellanies, The Works of Henry Fielding*, ed. Henry Knight Miller (Oxford: Oxford Univ. Press, 1972) 1: 84-117; Edward Burnaby Greene, *The Satires of Juvenal paraphrastically imitated and adapted to the Times. With a Preface* (London, 1763); *The Adulteress* (London, 1773).

12. Edward Owen, *The Satires of Juvenal, translated into English verse; with a Correct Copy of the Original Latin on the opposite Page; cleared of all the most exceptional Passages, and illustrated with marginal Notes from the Commentators* (London, 1785). All subsequent references to "A Looking-Glass for the Ladies" are to this text.

13. William Gifford, *The Satires of Decimus Junius Juvenalis. Translated into English Verse* (London, 1802), pp. 159-233.

14. *Critical Review*, no. 36, 2nd ser. (September, October, and November 1802).

15. William Gifford, *The Satires of Decimus Junius Juvenalis. Translated Into English Verse*, 2nd ed. (London, 1806). R.B. Clark, in *William Gifford: Tory Satirist, Critic, Editor* (New York: Columbia Univ. Press, 1931), gives a general description of the Gifford translations of Juvenal and Persius, as well as some critical responses.

16. *The Satires of Juvenal translated and illustrated by F. Hodgson* (London, 1807).

17. Dresses of that sort, Supple comments, are *"Rara avis in Terris, nigroque simillima Cygno.* That is, Madam, as much as to say, A rare Bird upon the Earth, and very like a black Swan." Henry Fielding, *The History of Tom Jones, a Foundling,* introduction by Martin C. Battestin, ed. Fredson C. Bowers (Oxford: Oxford Univ. Press, 1975), 1, bk. 4, Ch. 10.

CHAPTER VI

1. All citations of Swift's poems are from *The Poems of Jonathan Swift,* ed. Harold Williams, 2nd ed., rev., 3 vols. (Oxford: Oxford Univ. Press, 1958). "Strephon and Chloe" appears in 2: 584-93.

2. Denis Donoghue, *Jonathan Swift: A Critical Introduction* (Cambridge: Cambridge Univ. Press, 1969), pp. 191, 198.

3. William Law, *A Serious Call to a Devout and Holy Life, Adapted to the State and Condition of All Orders of Christians* (London, 1728), p. 93.

4. Ibid., p. 90.

5. Thomas Brown, *A Legacy for the Ladies, or Characters of the Women of the Age, with a Comical View of London and Westminster: Or, the Merry Quack* (London, 1705), p. 59.

6. *Irish Tracts, 1720-1723, and Sermons,* in Herbert Davis, ed., *Prose Works of Jonathan Swift* (Oxford: Blackwell, 1948), 9: 89.

7. Rochester, *Complete Poems,* p. 47.

8. Dryden, *Poems, 1693-1696*, pp. 145, 187.

9. *Mundus Muliebris, or the Ladies Dressing-Room Unlock'd, and the Toilette Spread. Together with the Fop-Dictionary* . . . (London, 1690), pp. 20-21.

10. François Bruys, *The Art of Knowing Women: or, the Female Sex Dissected, in a Faithful Representation of their Virtues and Vices . . . Written in French, by the Chevalier Plante-Amor, and by him published at the Hague, 1729* (London, 1730), p. 114. *L'Art de connaître des femmes* was translated by Spring Macky in 1730. A second edition was printed for Curll in 1732.

11. *Whipping Tom or A Rod for a Proud Lady, Bundled Up in Four Feeling Discourses, Both Serious and Merry*, 4th ed. (London, 1722), p. 22.

12. Edward Ward, *Female Policy Detected, or the Arts of a Designing Woman Lain Open in Works of Edward Ward* (London, 1695; rpt. 1761), p. 6. The work was much reprinted in the eighteenth century. Ward used Jacques Olivier, *Alphabet de l'Imperfections et Malice des Femmes* (1666), translated into English as *A Discourse of Women, Shewing their imperfections alphabetically. Newly translated out of the French into English* (London, 1662).

13. The reference appears in this title as listed in *A Bibliography of the Writings of Jonathan Swift*, ed. Arthur Scouten, rev. by Dr. H. Teerink, 2nd ed. (Philadelphia, 1963), p. 363. Entry 744 reads, "A / Beautiful / Young Nymph / Going to Bed. / Written for the Honour of the *Fair Sex*. / — / Pars minima est ipsa Puella sui. / Ovid. Remed. Amoris. . . ."

14. Ovid, *The Art of Love and Other Poems*, trans. J.H. Mozley, 2nd ed. rev. by G.P. Goold, Loeb Classical Library (Cambridge: Harvard Univ. Press, 1979), p. 201. All references to Ovid are to this edition.

15. For precedents see James Clifford's "A Beautiful Young Nymph Going to Bed," *Johnsonian Newsletter* 10 (February 1950): 7-8; Clarence Kulischeck, "Swift's Poems about Women," *JNL* 10 (May 1950): 11-12; Irvin Ehrenpreis, *The Personality of Jonathan Swift* (London: Methuen, 1958), pp. 32-46; and Bonamy Dobrée, *English Literature in the Early Eighteenth Century, 1700-1740* (Oxford: Clarendon Press, 1959), p. 463. Also see Harry Miller Solomon on "A Beautiful Young Nymph" in *Tennessee Studies in Literature* 22 (1977): 105-16, and on "The Lady's Dressing Room," *Studies in English Literature, 1500-1900* 19 (1979): 431-44. I agree with Solomon, who calls attention to popular verse satires and ballads to show that Swift's reader would recognize the genre as "one of the few survivors of a coarse and once flourishing tradition of scatological antifeminism."

16. Richard Ames's *The Folly of Love* (2nd ed., 1693; 4th ed., 1700), written in response to Robert Gould's *Satyr Against Women* (London, 1680), sparked a number of controversial satires discussed in chapter 1, above. Gould's later *Satyr Against Wooing* (1698), opening with a Juvenalian motto, similarly intrudes on a woman's boudoir to provide an antidote to love.

17. Katharine M. Rogers, "'My Female Friends': The Misogyny of Jonathan Swift," *Texas Studies in Language and Literature* 1 (1959): 379. More recently James Tyne, in "Swift and Stella: The Love Poems," *Tennessee Studies in Literature* 19 (1974): 36, labels Swift a misogynist. Peter Schakel in *The Poetry of Jonathan Swift: Allusion and the Development of a Poetic Style* (Madison: Univ.

of Wisconsin Press, 1978), has argued that the poems create an "impression of loss of control by a man who is trying to exhibit his self-control" (p. 119).

18. In a lively exchange of ideas, Ellen Pollak takes issue with Susan Gubar (see chapter 2, note 5, above). Pollak finds Swift's use of the "repulsive female" an emblem for his failure to accept the ambiguity of the human condition. Gubar gives little significance to the Juvenalian or Ovidian context and suggests that Swift's Christianity might even urge male readers to attend to women's Eve-like nature.

19. This concept reached its extreme in other tracts in which woman was portrayed as a cannibal or vulture who eats men (*Misogynus: Or A Satyr Upon Women* [London, 1682], p. 7), as a hand grenade to be tossed away before it explodes, or as a killer whore who carries deadly disease (Ned Ward, *Female Policy Detected*, pp. 20, 78).

20. John M. Aden, in "Corinna and the Sterner Muse of Swift," *English Language Notes* 4 (1966): 23-31, has called attention to "a composite of absurdity and pathos" aroused by Swift's use of "batter'd" and other appeals to sentiment. See also Aden's "Those Gaudy Tulips: Swift's 'Unprintables,'" in *Quick Springs of Sense: Studies in the Eighteenth Century*, ed. Larry Champion (Athens: Univ. of Georgia Press, 1974), pp. 15-32.

21. Donald Greene in "On Swift's 'Scatological' Poems," *Sewanee Review* 75 (1967): 672-89, shows that Strephon in "The Lady's Dressing Room" is in love with Celia's image, and Strephon becomes the appropriate victim of his own obsession. Greene stresses the theological implications of the poem and "Swift's view of love (which is also the view of the Gospels) as something that transcends the merely material, the physical, the self-regarding."

22. Ronald Paulson in "Swift, Stella, and Permanence," *ELH* 27 (1960): 298-314, contrasts the theme of the mutability of body and soul in the Stella poems to the dressing-room poems. John Irwin Fischer in *On Swift's Poetry* (Gainesville: Univ. of Florida Press, 1978), finds the Stella poems to be assertions of belief that urge Stella toward faith in her own salvation—part of his larger thesis that Swift brought his antagonisms under control through using his poems to reflect moral responsibility. In a briefer consideration, Nora Crow Jaffe, *The Poet Swift* (Hanover, N.H.: University Press of New England, 1977), generally argues that Swift's attitude to women, while sometimes inspired by dark pathology, aims away from condescension.

23. Jean Hagstrum, *Sex and Sensibility: Ideal and Erotic Love from Milton to Mozart* (Chicago: Univ. of Chicago Press, 1980), pp. 153-57, emphasizes that in Swift's poetry, Stella's body exists, though I am less convinced of Hagstrum's argument that Swift's poetry on women results from his deep psychic needs. I am, however, much indebted to Hagstrum's discussion of Swift's and Pope's women.

CHAPTER VII

1. Lord Lyttleton, *Advice to a Lady* (London, 1731).

2. *Female Chastity, Truth and Sanctity: A Satire* (London, 1735); *Swift's*

Vision: or, the Women's Hue and Cry Against Alexander Pope, for the Loss of their Characters (Dublin, 1757).

3. *Spectator,* II: 320-21.

4. Rae Blanchard, "Richard Steele and the Status of Women," *Studies in Philology* 36 (1929): 325-55. It is worth noting with Blanchard that "irrational and selfish women portrayed by Steele far outnumber those whose conduct is motivated by reason; the ideal woman—the Lady Sharlots, Eucratias and Indianas—exemplify the aspect of his 'anti-rationalism' which expressed itself, in this particular as in others, in a concept of sentimental virtue."

5. *Spectator,* IV: 18.

6. I have drawn from the attractive edition of the poetic fragment by Hugh Lloyd-Jones, *Females of the Species: Semonides on Women* (London: Noyes Press, 1975).

7. Walsh, *Dialogue Concerning Women,* p. 20.

8. *Females of the Species,* p. 54.

9. Other minor satires of limited interest are *The Female Rake, Female Faction* (1729), *Advice to the Ladies* (1730), and *Flowers of Parnassus* (1735).

10. *The Creation of Women: A Poem* (Dublin, 1725), p. 14.

11. Thomas Parnell, *Hesiod: or, The Rise of Woman, The Works in Verse and Prose of Dr. Thomas Parnell Late Arch-Deacon of Clogher, enlarged with variations and poems not before published* (Glasgow, 1755), p. 9.

12. Lady Mary Wortley Montagu, *Essays and Poems and "Simplicity, a Comedy,"* ed. Robert Halsband and Isobel Grundy (Oxford: Clarendon Press, 1977), p. 210. All subsequent references to the poem are to this edition. The poem is puzzling in part because Lady Mary attacks Swift's misogyny in an eight-page pamphlet, *The Dean's Provocation for Writing the Lady's Dressing Room* (1734). For other rejoinders to Swift, see Robert Halsband, "'The Lady's Dressing Room' Explicated by a Contemporary," in *The Augustan Milieu,* ed. H.K. Miller, Eric Rothstein, and G.S. Rousseau (Oxford: Clarendon Press, 1970), pp. 225-31.

13. Spence, MS. Eg. 2234, f. 248, cited in Robert Halsband, *The Life of Lady Mary Wortley Montagu* (Oxford: Clarendon Press, 1956), p. 85.

14. *Essays and Poems,* p. 133.

15. Robert Halsband, "'Condemned to Petticoats': Lady Mary Wortley Montague as Feminist and Writer," in *The Dress of Words: Essays on Restoration and Eighteenth-Century Literature in Honor of Richmond P. Bond,* ed. Robert B. White, Jr. (Manhattan: Univ. of Kansas Press, 1978), pp. 35-52, follows a similar argument for Lady Mary's feminism, though he does not mention the contradictory evidence of the Boileau translation.

16. *Complete Letters of Lady Mary Wortley Montagu,* ed. Robert Halsband (Oxford: Clarendon Press, 1965-67), 1: 68.

17. Ibid., pp. 90, 91, 99, 101, 143.

18. Ibid., p. 45.

19. To Lady Bute, 6 March 1753, ibid., 3: 27.

20. The text of Nicolas Boileau-Despréaux is in his *Oeuvres Complètes* 28, Bibliothèque de La Pléiade (Bruges: Sainte-Catherine, 1966), vol. 2.

21. [Autobiographical romance: fragment] in *Essays and Poems,* p. 79.

22. *Essays and Poems*, pp. 230-32. The poem is printed also in Isobel Grundy's discussion, "Ovid and Eighteenth-Century Divorce: An Unpublished Poem by Lady Mary Wortley Montagu," *Review of English Studies*, n.s. 23 (1972): 417-28.

23. *The Nonsense of Common-Sense*, No. VI (Tuesday, 17 January 1738), in *Essays and Poems*, p. 134. The essay was reprinted as "An Apology for the Ladies," *London Magazine*, January 1738.

24. Edward Young, *Love of Fame, the Universal Passion in Seven Characteristical Satires* in *Poetical Works of Edward Young* (1833; rpt. Westport, Conn.: Greenwood Press, 1970). All subsequent references to the poem are to this edition.

25. The fullest discussion of the poem is in Howard Weinbrot's *The Formal Strain: Studies in Augustan Imitation and Satire* (Chicago: Univ. of Chicago Press, 1969), pp. 113-28.

26. Weinbrot comments on the inefficacy of using a dash as a representation of a general ideal. In either case, as a generalized norm or a particular famous person, the device thwarts the power of the satire. See Weinbrot, *Formal Strain*, pp. 106-07.

27. Weinbrot notes that "Young is incapable of grasping either the presence of tragedy in his own poem, or the destructive power of the facile portrait of Caroline's goodness." *Formal Strain*, p. 125.

28. Marlene Le Gates, "The Cult of Womanhood in Eighteenth-Century Thought," *Eighteenth-Century Studies* 10 (1976): 21-39, finds that the emphasis shifts to an ideal virtuous woman attacked by an aggressive male. Women are still perceived as inherently dangerous and disorderly, but their taming becomes a tribute to the power of reason to shape human nature.

29. Montagu, *Essays and Poems*, p. 131.

CHAPTER VIII

1. See, for example, *The Rape of the Lock and Other Poems*, ed. Geoffrey Tillotson, Twickenham Edition, 3rd. ed., vol. 2 (New Haven: Yale Univ. Press, 1962). All subsequent references to *The Rape of the Lock* are to this edition. See also Arthur Hoffman, "Spenser and *The Rape of the Lock*," *Philological Quarterly* 49 (1970): 530-46; James L. Jackson, "Pope's *The Rape of the Lock* Considered as a Five-Act Epic," *PMLA* 64 (1950): 1283-87; Pat Rogers, "Faery Lore and *The Rape of the Lock*," *Review of English Studies*, n.s. 25 (1974): 25-38; and Aubrey Williams, "The 'Fall' of China and *The Rape of the Lock*," *Philological Quarterly* 41 (1962): 412-25.

2. *The Rape of the Lock*, 2: 142.

3. *A Satyr Upon Old Maids* (London, 1713), p. 12.

4. Walsh, *Dialogue Concerning Women*, p. 79.

5. Bruys, *Art of Knowing Women*, pp. ii, iv.

6. Elkin, *Augustan Defence of Satire*, p. 135 ff., gives numerous examples of eighteenth-century satirists who claimed to avoid references to specific individuals.

7. *Rape of the Lock*, 2: 180, iii.158.

8. For other references to lapdogs in "The Rape of the Lock," see i.15-16;

ii.110; iv.75; and iv.120. Ronald Paulson, *Popular and Polite Art in the Age of Hogarth and Fielding* (Notre Dame, Ind.: Univ. of Notre Dame Press, 1979), p. 54, notes the lapdog's appearance as the lover's surrogate in "Titian's *Venus of Urbino* in the Uffizi, Watteau's *Lady at Her Toilet* in the Wallace Collection, and Fragonard's *Le Guinblute* showing the dog hoisted in air between the lady's outspread legs."

9. Cleanth Brooks, "The Case of Miss Arabella Fermor" in *The Well Wrought Urn: Studies in the Structure of Poetry* (New York: Harcourt Brace, 1947), pp. 95-96.

10. Ralph Cohen, "Transformation in *The Rape of the Lock,*" *Eighteenth-Century Studies* 2 (1969): 205-24.

11. Hugo Reichard, "The Love Affair in Pope's *Rape of the Lock,*" *PMLA* 69 (1954): 888.

12. See Alexander Pope, *Minor Poems*, ed. Norman Ault, completed by John Butt (London: Methuen, 1964), 6: 63.

13. Brooks, "Case of Miss Arabella Fermor," p. 87. For an example of a reading which takes issue with Brooks, see Sheila Delaney, "Sex and Politics in Pope's *Rape of the Lock,*" *English Studies in Canada* 1 (1975): 46-61.

14. The quotation from Jean de La Bruyère is from "Les Caractères des Femmes," *Les Caractères de Théophraste traduits du grec avec Les Caractères ou les Moeurs de ce siècle* (Paris: Garnier, 1962), no. 53, p. 145.

15. *Epistles to Several Persons (Moral Essays),* ed. F.W. Bateson, Twickenham Edition (London: Methuen, 1950), III.ii.46-74. All references to "Epistle to a Lady" are to this edition. Rufa, Sappho, Calypso, Narcissa, the Queen, and assorted couplets derive from earlier compositions. See *Epistles to Several Persons,* III.ii.ix-lvii; and Frank Brady, "The History and Structure of Pope's *To A Lady,*" *Studies in English Literature, 1500-1900* 9 (1969): 439-62, for discussion of textual problems relating to the poem.

16. See Irvin Ehrenpreis's important essay, "The Cistern and the Fountain: Art and Reality in Pope and Gray," in *Studies in Criticism and Aesthetics, 1660-1800: Essays in Honor of Samuel Holt Monk,* ed. Howard Anderson and John S. Shea (Minneapolis: Univ. of Minnesota Press, 1967), pp. 156-75.

17. Patricia Meyer Spacks, *An Argument of Images: The Poetry of Alexander Pope* (Cambridge: Harvard Univ. Press, 1971), p. 158.

18. Richard Brinsley Sheridan, *Dramatic Works,* ed. Cecil Price (Oxford: Clarendon Press, 1973), 1: 338.

19. *Woman Not Inferior to Man or A Short and Modest Vindication of the Natural Right of the Fair Sex to a Perfect Equality of Power, Dignity, and Esteem with the Men* (London, 1739), p. 21. Sophia also published a response to *Man Superior to Woman, or a Vindication of Man's Natural Right of Sovereign Authority Over the Woman, In Answer to Sophia, by a Gentleman* [K.] (London, 1739), in 1740 entitled *Woman's Superior Excellence Over Man.*

20. Lady Mary Chudleigh, *Essays Upon Several Subjects in Prose and Verse* (London, 1710), p. 173.

21. Brown, *Legacy for the Ladies,* pp. 2-4.

22. *Spectator,* 2: 9-10.

23. Law, *A Serious Call,* p. 97.

24. Bruys, *Art of Knowing Women,* p. 82. He distinguishes male self-love from female: "This same Self-Love is so irradicably grafted in the Female-Sex, that they seem to imagine they had a real Right of imposing on all Mankind an implicit Belief of their Imaginary Excellencies and pretended Merit" (p. 18).

25. Brown, *Legacy for the Ladies,* p. 31.

26. The remarks appear in an undated letter [1749] from Mrs. Montagu to Mrs. Donellan transcribed in *The R.B. Adams Library Relating to Dr. Samuel Johnson* (London: Oxford Univ. Press, 1929), 3: 173.

27. Bodleian Library Ballard MS. 43.f.155. That women despise women and thus themselves is also a commonplace. In Swift's "Letter to a Young Lady," *Irish Tracts, 1720-1723, and Sermons,* ed. Herbert Davis, vol. 9 of *Prose Works of Jonathan Swift* (Oxford: Blackwell, 1948), p. 88, Swift writes that he "never yet knew a tolerable Woman to be fond of her own sex." And Laetitia Pilkington, a woman sometimes tolerable to Swift, in her *Memoirs* (see chapter 2, note 2, above), p. 108, regrets that "what I think most surprising, is, that Women, who have suffered in their own Reputations, are generally most cruel in their Censure on others."

28. The poem, appearing in the *General Advertiser* (16 March 1751), was provoked by the publication of Tobias Smollett's *Peregrine Pickle,* which included Lady Jane Vane's "Memoirs of a Lady of Quality." It is also in the Bodleian Library Ballard MS. 37.f.28.

29. *The Female Mentor or Select Conversations* (London, 1793), 1: 132.

30. James Fordyce, *Sermons to Young Women,* 3rd American ed. from 12th London ed. (1766; rpt. Philadelphia: M. Carey, 1809), pp. 215-16. Samuel Johnson contributed the preface to this book.

31. Young, *Love of Fame,* p. 113. See also Charlotte Crawford, "What Was Pope's Debt to Edward Young?" *ELH* 13 (1946): 157-67.

32. See Rebecca Parkin, "The Role of Time in Alexander Pope's 'Epistle to a Lady'," *ELH* 32 (1965): 490-501, for a thorough exploration of the persistent moral crises occasioned by the ladies' transience. According to Parkin, tension arises between the apparent leisurely pace of the speaker and the fleeting time which destroys women's beauty.

33. *Spectator* No. 242 (7 December 1711), II: 443.

34. *Spectator* No. 37 (12 April 1711), I: 152-58.

35. Frank Brady in "History and Structure of Pope's 'To A Lady'" suggests that the Atossa portrait should immediately follow Philomedé, though this creates a question of the appropriate antecedent for "these" ("But what are these to great Atossa's Mind?"). The portrait makes sense where it is, with "these" referring to the previous five fools. Atossa as "the wisest fool much Time has ever made" is thus a suitable climax to Pope's portrait of the fools.

36. Paulson, "Swift, Stella, and Permanence," pp. 298-314.

37. See Pope's letter to Swift, 16 February 1732/33: "Your Lady friend is *Semper Eadem,* and I have written an Epistle to her on that qualification in a female character." *The Correspondence of Alexander Pope,* ed. George Sherburn (Oxford: Clarendon Press, 1956), 3: 349.

38. The light imagery in the passage includes lines revised from Pope's 1722 poem to Judith Cowper. Pope substitutes "orb" for "sun," "when" for "while," etc., but most significant is the change from "in virgin majesty" to "in virgin Modesty." Majestic queenliness would have suggested that Martha Blount might long to be queen for life.

39. *Minor Poems*, p. 62.

40. *Man Superior to Woman*, p. 73.

41. William Ayre, *Memoirs of the Life and Writings of Alexander Pope* (London, 1745), 2: 52-53, cited in *Epistles to Several Persons*, III.ii.68.

42. Owen Ruffhead, *Life of Pope* (London, 1769), p. 285.

43. Spacks, *Argument of Images*, p. 167.

44. Jean Hagstrum in *Sex and Sensibility*, pp. 141-42, emphasizes Blount's virginal qualities, her separation from the corporeal, as Pope portrays her.

CHAPTER IX

1. Lillian Bloom and Edward Bloom, "The Satiric Mode of Feeling: A Theory of Intention," *Criticism* 11 (1969): 117. See also their *Satire's Persuasive Voice* (Ithaca: Cornell Univ. Press, 1979); and Peter Elkin, *Augustan Defence of Satire*.

2. See especially Jean Hagstrum, *Sex and Sensibility*, to whom I am indebted for his discussion of *angélisme*.

3. Thomas Lockwood, *Post-Augustan Satire: Charles Churchill and Satirical Poetry, 1750-1800* (Seattle: Univ. of Washington Press, 1979); W.B. Carnochan, "Satire, Sublimity, and Sentiment: Theory and Practice in Post-Augustan Satire," *PMLA* 85 (1970): 260-67.

4. Peter Hughes, "Reconstructing Literary History: Implications for the Eighteenth Century," *New Literary History* 8 (1977): 269.

5. Marlene LeGates argues that traditional misogyny was "replaced" by the image of the "chaste maiden and obedient wife" in "The Cult of Womanhood in Eighteenth-Century Thought," *Eighteenth-Century Studies* 10 (1977): 21-39.

6. For a fine discussion of the legal status of the fallen woman, see Susan Staves, "British Seduced Maidens," *Eighteenth-Century Studies* 14 (1980): 109-34.

7. Bod. Ms. Add. d. 89.f.29, cited in William H. Epstein, *John Cleland: Images of a Life* (New York: Columbia Univ. Press, 1974), p. 98.

8. *The Female Congress* (1779), p. vii, a lengthy poem in the collection of the Henry E. Huntington Library, San Marino, California, was probably written by William Preston and is loosely based on Juvenal's Sixth Satire.

9. Richard Polwhele, *The Unsex'd Females, A Poem, Addressed to the Author of the Pursuits of Literature* (1798), in Gina Luria, ed., *The Feminist Controversy in England, 1788-1810* (New York: Garland, 1974), p. 9.

10. *Female Virtues: A Poem* (London, 1787) and *The Female Aegis, or the Duties of Women from Childhood to Old Age*, in Luria, *Feminist Controversy*.

11. See Jean Hunter, "'The Ladies Magazine' and the History of the Eighteenth-Century Englishwoman," in *Newsletters to Newspapers: Eighteenth-*

Century Journalism, ed. Donovan H. Bond and W. Reynolds McLeod (Morgantown, W. Va.: West Virginia Univ. Press, 1977), pp. 103-18.

12. Neil McKendrick, "Home Demand and Economic Growth: A New View of the Role of Women and Children in the Industrial Revolution," *Historical Perspectives: Studies in English Thought and Society in Honour of J.H. Plumb,* ed. Neil McKendrick (London: Europa, 1974), p. 167. See also Eric Richards, "Women in the British Economy Since about 1700: An Interpretation," *History* 59 (1974): 337-57, who argues that the Industrial Revolution was not to the advantage of women.

13. Barbara B. Schnorrenberg and Jean H. Hunter, "The Eighteenth-Century Englishwoman," in *The Women of England from Anglo-Saxon Times to the Present,* ed. Barbara Kanner (Hamden, Conn.: Shoe String Press, 1979), pp. 183-228. Also included is an excellent bibliography.

14. Mary Wollstonecraft, *A Vindication of the Rights of Woman,* ed. Carol H. Poston, Norton Critical Edition (New York: W.W. Norton, 1975), p. 138.

15. Ibid., p. 27.

16. Ibid., pp. 95, 52 n.8.

Index